Catherine **JEANNOT**

L'Anglais en entreprise

• • •

100 situations et les mots pour le dire

A manual and tool intended for personal assistants working in an international environment and using advanced English as their language of communication.

ÉDITIONS OPHRYS

CHEZ LE MÊME ÉDITEUR

- *L'anglais du management,* Katia TANANT
- *Manuel d'anglais de la bourse et de la finance,* Michel VAN DER YEUGHT
- *L'anglais de la bourse et de la finance : description et recherche,* Michel VAN DER YEUGHT

Direction éditoriale : Alexandra Lepinay
Suivi éditorial : Sarah Funel
Couverture : Cécile Hébrard
Maquette et mise en page : Interscript

Éditions OPHRYS
1, rue du Bac, 75007 Paris
www.ophrys.fr

ISBN 978-2-7080-1388-9

GENÈSE

Cet ouvrage est né de la fascination de l'auteur pour la langue anglaise, ses infinies possibilités et sa capacité à dire avec tant de précision et d'inventivité. Observatrice du comportement des mots, ceux qui s'attirent et ceux qui se fuient, et convaincue de l'importance du mot juste, son bagage de linguiste et de pédagogue a largement coloré la fonction qu'elle a exercée en tant qu'assistante bilingue. Tout naturellement, quatre parties du présent ouvrage sont introduites dans cette même langue. Les chapitres sont replacés dans leur contexte et rédigés en anglais : anecdotes, exemples et expériences parfois pittoresques éclairent à la fois le contenu lexical et la fonction de l'assistant(e).

La vocation de cet ouvrage est d'être un outil pour une bonne communication là où l'anglais est la langue ressource. C'est aussi de partager les trésors d'une langue qui résiste aux assauts du « Globish » et qui ne cesse de livrer ses richesses. Enjoy!

AVANT PROPOS

Le quotidien en entreprise nous plonge dans des situations où le discours que nous tenons et les mots que nous utilisons échappent aux phrases apprivoisées et parfaitement limées de nos manuels. Dans un contexte international, l'assistant bilingue, plaque tournante de l'entreprise, se trouve au centre d'échanges multiples dans lesquels sa capacité à communiquer est un atout et un enjeu majeur : à situations diversifiées et parfois complexes, expressions adaptées et nuancées ! Le présent ouvrage témoigne de cette diversité qui fait alterner des registres et des niveaux de langue différents, passant de l'argot au technique, du familier au formel, de l'humoristique au protocolaire.

Loin des clichés et au plus près de ce qui se dit dans les bureaux il propose de parcourir un arsenal de locutions dont l'anglophone dispose et use au fil des jours en entreprise. Elles ont été recueillies, puis classées par thème et type d'activité. Elles accompagneront donc ***l'assistant(e) bilingue*** et ***l'office manager***, les ***étudiants*** du BTS assistant manager et assistant de direction et ***toute personne appelée à communiquer*** efficacement en anglais dans un milieu international.

Si cet ouvrage est une invitation à savourer l'inventivité et le génie de la langue anglaise, il est également un OUTIL :

Conçu pour les utilisateurs d'un niveau intermédiaire ou avancé

- Il propose la traduction, entière ou partielle, de la majorité des 1500 phrases sélectionnées, mais évite le mot à mot afin de restituer un français authentique.
  - examinons cet exemple p. 57 :
    - May we take this opportunity to remind participants that ***we'll be wrapping up the meeting at 4 o'clock sharp***/on the dot?
      ➛ *nous terminerons notre réunion à 4 heures précises.*

Les mots sélectionnés en gras correspondent à la phrase traduite en français et en rouge. La barre oblique signale une alternative. Dans cet exemple, substituer "on the dot" à "sharp" offrirait un sens équivalent : "we'll be wrapping up the meeting at 4 o'clock on the dot."

- Il laisse le lecteur apprécier là où le sens est limpide et le français absent :
  - un simple jeu de prépositions par exemple,
    - I'll pass this information along to our team members.
    - Could you e-mail your CV over to us?
  - ou le jeu des collocations
    - Your presence would be greatly appreciated.
  - ou le ton
    - Welcome and please let me know if you should need anything at all!
    - I'd be happy to forward your CV to the Human Resources department.
- Il contient des expressions contemporaines originaires du français (« on est au taquet », « c'est une vraie usine à gaz ») ou de l'anglais – majoritairement britannique ("step up to the plate").

Des expressions en contexte

- Chacune des phrases ayant été recueillie en situation, les 1500 entrées apparaissent toujours en contexte. Ceci permet :
  - un sens plus clair
    - ***Let me repeat that back to you and check I've got the correct address.***
      ➛ *Je répète et vérifie que j'ai bien noté l'adresse.*
    - I will be ***on call*** if there's an emergency and you need to get hold of me.
      ➛ *d'astreinte*
  - la pérennité de la tournure, puisqu'elle pourra être réactivée dans des contextes analogues.

Un anglais idiomatique, contemporain et opérationnel

- Il est directement recueilli à la source.

MODE D'EMPLOI

L'ouvrage s'organise en **cinq parties dont quatre** répondent aux enjeux du métier d'assistant bilingue et aux différentes facettes de ses fonctions.

PARTIE I

LE QUOTIDIEN DE L'ASSISTANT(E) apporte des outils pour communiquer sur des questions d'ordre organisationnel et administratif.

1. Exemples d'utilisation :
   - À l'occasion d'un séminaire, je dois indiquer à mes hôtes d'outre-Atlantique la marche à suivre pour leur accès à notre site.
     - je me reporte à la table des matières et je choisis la partie qui correspond à ma problématique LE QUOTIDIEN DE L'ASSISTANTE/SÉMINAIRES (PART ONE/CHAPTER 6).
     - je sélectionne ORGANISATION ET PREPARATIFS (p. 55) et je consulte la rubrique Liste des participants et badges (p. 56).
       - ***You are invited to sign in upon arrival at the reception desk.***

         ➛ *Vous êtes invité à vous enregistrer à l'accueil dès votre arrivée.*
   - Autre exemple : Je dois réparer une maladresse :
     - je me reporte dans la table des matières et je choisis LE QUOTIDIEN DE L'ASSISTANTE/AGENDAS ET REUNIONS (PART ONE/CHAPTER 1).
     - je sélectionne DE LA NUANCE AU TACT (p. 20) puis je consulte la rubrique REVENIR SUR UNE ERREUR OU UNE MALADRESSE (p. 23).
       - ***Having re-read my last mail***, it seemed to me that my remark on "..." was unfortunately followed by "....". No offence intended.

         ➛ *Après relecture de mon dernier mail*
2. Le chapitre AUTOUR DU TEMPS fait un gros plan sur les expressions relatives au temps, souvent problématiques pour le locuteur français. Par souci d'efficacité, il est présenté sous forme de lexique dont la langue de départ est le français. Il s'utilise comme un dictionnaire français/anglais.

- Je suis en région parisienne et mon collègue hollandais doit prendre le Thalys. Je crains qu'il n'ait pas prévu assez de marge pour sa correspondance RER-Thalys :
    - je me reporte à la table des matières et je choisis AUTOUR DU TEMPS (PART ONE/CHAPTER 2).
    - je sélectionne COORDINATION (p. 34) puis je consulte la rubrique MARGE (p. 35).
    - – ***You might be cutting it fine.***
      ➢ *C'est peut-être prévoir un peu juste/ça ne vous laisse pas beaucoup de marge.*

PARTIE II

BIEN PARLER ET MENUS PROPOS a pour objectif la communication en vue de créer du lien d'une part et de faciliter les échanges d'idées d'autre part.

Exemples d'utilisation :

- Je suis en possession de documents qui, semble-t-il, sont adressés à une autre personne :
    - je me reporte à la table des matières et je choisis BIEN PARLER ET MENUS PROPOS/METTRE EN RELATION (PART TWO/CHAPTER 2).
    - je sélectionne et je consulte SERVIR D'INTERMEDIAIRE (p. 87 et 88).
    - – ***It came about that I received a request which I believe was meant for you.***
      ➢ *Il se trouve que j'ai reçu une demande qui, me semble-t-il, vous était adressée.*
- Mon supérieur hiérarchique m'a chargé(e) de rédiger une lettre de recommandation :
    - je me reporte à la table des matières et je choisis BIEN PARLER ET MENUS PROPOS/RH ET COMMUNICATION (PART TWO/CHAPTER 5).
    - je sélectionne LE CANDIDAT ET SON CV (p. 109) et je consulte la rubrique ÊTRE RECOMMANDÉ PAR SON RESPONSABLE (p. 111).
    - – *She **has won her colleagues' trust** and has become indispensable to the team.*
      ➢ *a su gagner la confiance de ses collègues*

PARTIE III

365 LOCUTIONS AU FIL DES JOURS, (autant de jours dans l'année plus une pour les années bissextiles !) est une partie construite autour des centaines d'expressions qui ponctuent notre discours, que nous bavardions devant la machine à café ou prenions la parole lors de réunions. Formules souvent imagées qui marquent notre appartenance à une même culture tant elles sont comprises de tous, justes et percutantes. Leur traduction en langue étrangère est souvent malaisée et parfois ne débouche que sur une expression équivalente.

Exemples d'utilisation :

- Feuilleter et savourer : les expressions et idiomes sont empruntés à l'une et l'autre langue et le lecteur épris du jeu des mots entre eux, en anglais comme en français, pourra la consulter à loisir.
- La recherche ciblée : je souhaite, par exemple, utiliser l'expression « c'est une évidence » :
  - j'ai recours à l'index et recherche « évidence ». Il me renvoie alors aux pages 80, 124 et 127. L'expression que je trouve adéquate se trouve page 127.

You can see that with half an eye

They are playing for time. You can see that with half an eye.
➛ *Ils essaient de gagner du temps. Cela saute aux yeux/ c'est une évidence.*

PARTIE IV

RESTONS CALMES, est inspirée de la vie au bureau, avec les contraintes de la vie en équipe, les contrariétés, voire l'exaspération qu'elle génère fort bien connues notamment de l'assistant(e)… Les états d'âme peuvent s'exprimer alors « avec ou sans gants ». Face à ces situations, le locuteur dispose d'une palette riche pour exprimer tour à tour l'agacement, l'ironie, l'humour, le détachement, y mêler le bon sens ou un esprit vengeur. Le **glossaire** aide à en apprécier la teneur.

Qui dit vie au bureau, dit allées et venues dans les couloirs et aux étages, échanges entre deux portes, horaires et pointage, emplois du temps de ministre, rangements, etc. C'est l'objet du Chapitre 2 de cette partie. Les expressions étant organisées par thème, il est aisé de mener une recherche lexicale et de s'orienter.

Exemple d'utilisation :

- Si je suis surchargée et ne peux décemment pas accepter de traiter un nouveau dossier :
  - je me reporte à la table des matières et je choisis LA VIE AU BUREAU dans RESTONS CALMES (PART FOUR/CHAPTER 2).
  - je sélectionne et je consulte EMPLOIS DU TEMPS DE MINISTRE (p. 203, 204 et 205).
    - ***I'm a bit up against it, actually, so I'll have to put this on the back burner for the time being.***
      ➛ *Ça ne va pas être facile/je suis un peu charrette ; pour l'instant, je ne vais pas en faire une priorité.*

PARTIE V

À vous maintenant ! : huit textes narratifs à trous, une boîte à outils dans laquelle puiser pour les compléter. Le contexte ? Soirées cocktail mondaines, réservations de salle pas toujours commodes, prises de fonction mouvementées, conflits sociaux inquiétants et péripéties diverses. Le temps est venu maintenant pour le lecteur de partir à l'assaut de nouveaux contextes. Testez votre capital lexical engrangé au fil des chapitres. La démarche est simple, il s'agit de retrouver dans l'encart situé en tête de chaque histoire les termes et locutions correspondant aux espaces vidés de leur contenu. Guidé dans cet exercice, vous restituez au texte tout son sens à mesure que l'histoire se déroule. Façon plaisante de mobiliser vos connaissances tout en vous imprégnant d'un anglais contemporain et vivant. Les clés se trouvent en fin de partie.

INDEX ET GLOSSAIRE

À tout instant il est possible de consulter l'**index** : il renvoie à toutes les occurrences du mot français recherché. Ces mots apparaissent dans différents contextes éclairés par les éléments de traduction utiles à la compréhension.

Le **glossaire** est un support à la compréhension. Le mot ou l'expression y est traduit dans la forme et le sens précis de la phrase dans laquelle il se trouve.

REMERCIEMENTS

Je remercie John Gilroy, de l'Université Anglia Ruskin à Cambridge, mon professeur et ami, pour sa disponibilité de tous les instants et pour ses encouragements.

Merci à Rémi, mon époux, pour ses conseils judicieux et son soutien enthousiaste, diligent et inconditionnel.

Merci à Yvonne Gibson et Françoise Bastien qui m'ont accompagnée dans ma quête du mot juste.

L'idée de cet ouvrage n'aurait jamais germé cependant sans notre longue conversation cet après-midi de juillet à West Ruislip… T'en souvient-il Estelle ?

TABLE OF CONTENTS

PART TWO

KEY – CORRIGÉS

PROLOGUE

This is the book I would have liked to find when I set out to become a bilingual executive assistant and was scanning the shelves of the many bookshops I visited. There are some excellent books out there, based on first-hand experience of the corporate world, and first-class guides that give invaluable information on how to write and communicate effectively in any industry. Many of these I bought and used as reliable tools for my daily correspondence, presentations, translations and seminar preparation material.

None however, served the dual purpose of holding a mirror up to the realities of life as an assistant and of taking readers on a linguistic voyage through the corporate landscape.

My own journey took me to various companies for which I worked in a secretarial capacity, be it as sales, personal or executive assistant. A keen observer of the English language and of word behaviour, I have always kept a log, and every piece of natural spoken or written English I encountered has eventually found its way into it.

The collection I assembled now forms the bulk of my database. In the context of an international company, users can draw from it to address the wide variety of situations where English is a vehicle of clear business communication. They can make their way through this compilation of speech patterns, idioms and phrases, and take their pick as best suits their needs, replicate them and tailor them to the message they want to convey.

This book also aims to avoid falling in with the writing or speaking habits of jargon-hardened employees and intends to steer clear of 'globish' talk. It attempts to reflect the spirit and inventiveness of the English language which transcends the limitations imposed by the demands of the business environment.

Catherine Jeannot

GENERAL INTRODUCTION

English evolves and adapts. Its dominant presence on the business scene worldwide causes it to shift and develop. Bilingual executive or personal assistants, too, must have this capacity to absorb change and respond swiftly and inventively.

What is expected from them is not only practicality, but also resourcefulness and a capability to think outside the box. The seemingly simple task of scheduling the executive's appointments, requires good organisational skills as well as forward planning abilities, a good measure of common sense and of course tact, since other participants are involved. Technical knowledge, therefore, must be combined with the 'soft skills' that are so important when working in partnership with a boss, within a team environment and when working with clients. This has an impact on the use of language.

Part One is based on this observation. Both what you say, and how diplomatically you say it, matters. To discriminate shades of meaning has more than marginal relevance. A keen sense of the social nuances of the office enhances efficiency, so does courtesy and consideration towards others (otherwise known as 'Comity'). Many of the phrases I collected through listening to people and reading e-mails, offer good illustrations of this. The user will be able to choose phrases ranging from the straightforward 'no frills' practical, to the more complex and sophisticated.

Part One also includes a "<u>Time</u>" section. It was devised with the French speaker in mind. Time and timing are at the heart of the assistant's activity when setting up timetables and meetings, and this is when the non-native English speaker is most starkly reminded that time-related expressions can be fiendishly difficult to translate. This section uses French as the source language and can be used in very much the same way as a bilingual dictionary.

Part Two is about communication on a need-to-know basis (Clarifying, Mapping out the future) and on a need-to-interact basis (Connecting people, Being positive, Facilitators, HR and Communication).

Part Three is more language-oriented, and focuses on phraseology and word patterns in a variety of situations involving boardroom meetings or off the record and informal snatches of conversation held while waiting at coffee machines. All 365 of the phrases that feature in it – one for each day to the avid user – are drawn from everyday office life and have naturally found their way under the heading "A phrase a day". For good measure, there is even an extra phrase for the leap year!

Part Four is devoted to the assistant's ability to keep as many balls in the air as possible and to be resilient under stress ("Keep your hair on").

"Office life" is full of the idiomatic English that people speak routinely in the office as a normal part of their jobs. It offers a selection of some of the turns of phrase they use in work-related situations or within the context of informal social interaction among colleagues.

Words matter, they are empowering agents in the workplace where so much depends on good communication and the easy flow of information. They are essential in ensuring that a "company" for which and with which employees work is able to live up to its original purpose ("cum pane", sharing the bread).

In **Part Five** called "**Write Your Own**", users are invited to try out their own expertise. Eight short stories based on anecdotes about real business life situations provide exciting opportunities to explore further contexts in which the words collected in the present book can be used. The 500-word-long stories can be completed by filling in the gaps with the appropriate word or group of words drawn from the tool box. Answers can then be checked against the complete story at the end of the section.

... PART ONE ...

Clerical functions
Le quotidien de l'assistant(e)

INTRODUCTION

Coordinating appointments or adjusting timetables engages personal assistants in exchanges of mails that can lead to endless strings of messages. The phrases collected in Part One say it all: the back and forth exchanges before setting a final date for an appointment, the time difference to be taken into account, the search for consensus, the need for flexibility. Sometimes circumstances dictate that decisions be made within a punishingly short timeframe: these are commonly known as "times of crisis". They result in the rapid firing and counter fire of e-mail messaging and hurried phone calls. Nowhere is this better illustrated than in the context of travel arrangements. The section devoted to "Travelling" contains entries that cover the key stages in the organisation and follow-through of business trips. They were culled from that plethora of e-mails that steadily accumulate in the personal assistant's mail box sometimes until unmanageable levels are reached.

Patience is an invaluable ally to personal assistants when dealing with requests, whether for passes, room reservations, computer hardware or software, SecurIDs, Blackberries, headphones or wiring equipment. It is a quality that will be tested to the nth degree. Once set in train the processes often grind on and stall. Whether on account of an application being momentarily disrupted or provider services stretched to their limit, the personal assistant has to be prepared to contend with delays, unanswered calls, and make repeated errands along corridors in a bid to cut down on waiting time. This of course, involves more legwork than linguistic prowess. A good number of phrases routinely used by assistants when dealing with requests make up a sizeable portion of Part one.

There are other sources of frustrations to the personal assistant, of course; procedures would be to name just one. These can be irritatingly ponderous. And the complexities of hiring extras are no exception. The slightest error or technicality will cause delays or throw the whole approval process off course. In the business cycle both the legal and sales departments are key. The contracts are drawn and documents provided to meet both their criteria. Taking shortcuts, therefore, is a guaranteed way to trouble.

However, Project Leaders' eagerness to make sure their teams are one consultant stronger and everyone prepared is not always matched by their grip of legal matters. Sometimes they show misplaced disdain for detail. The assistant's role then is to gain as high a level of accuracy as possible and to look out for anything that may set back the approval process or delay the jurist's signature. He or she must step in and check if all the relevant data are duly noted down in order that they can be fed into the software. In this context, a kind reminder to the members of the team may prove a sensible option. Phrases to that effect have found their way into Part One, too.

Timetables and meetings

Agendas et réunions

I. STARTER POINTS | BOÎTE À OUTILS

a) Coordinating an appointment
Mettre en place un rendez-vous

I would like ***to align with you*** and ask for your assistance in reconfirming the date on which we agreed.

➛ *me caler sur vous, me conformer à vos dates*

What would be good times for you on those two days?

➛ *Quels moments vous conviendraient*

We ought to ***shuffle dates around***, in order for Arnold to meet all his area managers and maximise his time during his visit in the US.

➛ *remanier/réorganiser les dates*

If scheduling permits, perhaps Michael could join us.

➛ *Selon l'emploi du temps/les horaires*

He is down to attend the presentation on biotechnology, and at the same time he is down to meet Mr Langham. Isn't there something we can do about the clash?

➛ *Il est inscrit comme participant à*

I am a little confused with the meeting planner as ***it comes across*** that I need to be in two places at once.

➛ *il apparaît que*

Could you please coordinate agendas and schedule a 60 minute telephone meeting?

I want to put these meetings on people's calendars ***to reserve the slots***. If you can let me have the list of ***attendees***, I'll send out the invites, unless, of course, you were planning on doing that yourself.
➛ *pour réserver les créneaux [...] participants*

You and I are on the same page, so we can move on and decide what the next step is going to be.
➛ *Nous sommes en phase/sur la même longueur d'onde*

How many people will make up the party? Let me know ***in good time***, so that I can be sure of a table.
➛ *suffisamment à l'avance*

Allow sufficient time for Richard to get from one end of the site to the other
➛ *Prévoyez large pour que Richard*

Let's make our arrangements nearer the time he is due to arrive.
➛ *Attendons d'être plus près de sa date d'arrivée pour nous organiser.*

Can't you ***find a gap*** in your diary? Celeste would really like to meet you.
➛ *trouver un créneau*

I'll contact you ***in due course***, when plans have been finalised.
➛ *en temps utile*

Please be aware that ***I have scheduled in*** an appointment with you for tomorrow.
➛ *j'ai planifié/prévu*

They service cars only by appointment, what dates would suit you best?
➛ *Les révisions de voitures ne se font que sur rendez-vous*

Then we'll take it from there, and schedule it in.
➛ *Ensuite on avisera et on l'intègrera dans l'emploi du temps.*

The diary commitments he has scheduled either side of his interview are extremely time consuming. He won't be able to travel back before 7 pm.

➛ *Avec les deux rendez-vous qu'il a prévus juste avant et juste après l'entretien, il ne disposera pas de beaucoup de temps.*

I'm calling to see ***if I can book myself in for a quick chat*** with Samir.

➛ *s'il reste une place pour un rapide entretien avec*

If you gave us prior notice, we could free up the evening and meet for dinner.

➛ *Si vous nous en informiez à l'avance*

I haven't heard back from Janet yet. ***When she gets back to us on the proposed timeslot, we'll settle for something.***

➛ *Lorsqu'elle nous donnera sa réponse pour l'horaire proposé, nous déciderons.*

I've put the question to him. ***I expect to hear back from him within a couple of days.***

➛ *Je pense qu'il reprendra contact d'ici quelques jours.*

I found your phone number through a circuitous route; finally I'm able to get hold of you!

➛ *J'ai enfin réussi à trouver votre numéro de téléphone.*

I think you are ***the person I should be contacting***.

➛ *la bonne personne, l'interlocuteur(-trice) que je recherche.*

I believe you are ***the person to put me in touch with*** the relevant department/the person who can make it happen.

➛ *la personne susceptible de m'aiguiller vers*

I'm calling ***on behalf of*** Mr Rolland who would like to know if you're aware of the fact that Friday is a bridge day in France/ at the urging of/at the behest of.

➛ *de la part de*

This is a brief call to ***bring you up to speed with*** the latest ESTA requirements.
➛ *vous mettre au courant de*

b) Suggesting a time
Proposer une heure

I also ***have some availability*** in the afternoon if lunch doesn't work.
➛ *j'ai des disponibilités/créneaux libres*

We will be sending ***a "save the date" invitation*** to external invitees.
➛ *une invitation pour retenir provisoirement la date*

After looking in his calendar, Christian would like me to inform you that 11 am would be ***the best available time*** for him.
➛ *l'heure à laquelle il est le mieux à même de se libérer/qui lui conviendrait le mieux.*

Could you ***give some notice if and when you're coming***?
➛ *confirmer à l'avance votre venue et dans ce cas l'heure de votre arrivée ?*

It might be a good idea to ***pencil in*** this date/this event in your diary awaiting confirmation.
➛ *noter provisoirement*

Don't forget that Pamela ***will be stopping by and is scheduled in for the end of the day***.
➛ *passera et est notée pour la fin de journée.*

Shall we aim to meet at 11.30 am?
➛ *Fixons-nous 11 h 30 comme heure de rendez-vous.*

We have to fix a time/***set a time for*** our next meeting, let's strike while the iron is hot/there's no time like the present.
➛ *fixer une heure*

c) Suggesting a date
Proposer une date

Are you available just now so I can ***take you through the org charts*** and explain the constraints and challenges?
➣ *vous commenter les organigrammes*

When we have all the replies we'll be able to ***lock in*** the meeting days.
➣ *bloquer/inscrire définitivement les jours de réunion.*

Please keep 8 June as a placeholder in your calendar.
➣ *Veuillez réserver la date du 8 juin*

Please put a hold on that date. I'll get back to you with specific meeting times.
➣ *Veuillez réserver cette date.*

I am sending this invitation for you to ***tentatively hold this date*** on your calendars.
➣ *réserver cette date de façon provisoire*

Keep those dates free/set those dates aside/retain those days/ ***until further notice.***
➣ *Assurez-vous que ces dates restent disponibles/ne prenez aucun rendez-vous jusqu'à nouvel ordre.*

Can you please ***advise if you have any time that day to*** meet with Stephan?
➣ *me signaler un éventuel créneau ce jour-là pour*

Would Luke be available on the following dates ***to speak to him in person*** for an hour: October 5,9,14,23?
➣ *pour le rencontrer en personne*

We are trying to organize the kick-off meeting, likely in Vitry, and ***we are shooting for*** a half day meeting.
➣ *et nous visons une demi-journée de réunion*

Should you want to talk through the options, I also have some availability in the afternoon if lunch doesn't work. I await your news.
➛ *Si vous souhaitez discuter du détail des options possibles/voir l'éventail des choix qui s'offrent à nous*

Can we make some forward plans: when are we going to meet again?
➛ *Il serait bon de nous projeter dans l'avenir*

I would be pleased if you could let me know your thoughts. ***Let's hook up soon/***let's make a point of getting together soon.
➛ *On s'appelle/on se voit bientôt ?/on reprend contact ?*

d) Offering/requesting a service
Offrir/demander un service

I am happy to help with any ***local arrangements***.
➛ *l'organisation sur place.*

Please ***have your assistant send me*** your logistics and I will arrange your accommodation.
➛ *faites-moi transmettre par votre assistante*

Can I please request your assistance in suggesting a restaurant and securing a reservation for Ram?
➛ *Auriez vous la gentillesse de*

If I can be of any help, don't hesitate to let me know.

Should you require further assistance, I'm available.

If you have any problems, please feel free to contact me.

If you need help, ***give me a shout***.
➛ *faites moi signe.*

e) Recurring meetings
Planifier une réunion récurrente

This meeting planner is to enable you to ***touch base with*** Amanda every month for 30 minutes.

➛ *faire un point avec*

I have currently set up the meeting to be held on the third Thursday of every month at 8.30 am. If this time does not work for you, please let me know.

➛ *Pour l'instant, j'ai fixé la réunion au troisième jeudi de chaque mois*

This meeting with Martin is ***a long-standing arrangement that still holds***: could you renew it on my Outlook Calendar for the next two months?

➛ *un dispositif mis en place de longue date et encore en vigueur*

f) Changing an appointment (time or date)
Modifier un RV (heure ou date)

Amanda, ***I am extending the call to half an hour*** based on experience of the duration of previous calls.

➛ *je porte à une demi-heure la durée de notre rendez-vous téléphonique*

I'm extending the call as experience has shown that a quarter of an hour was too short. We can shorten it if necessary but at least ***we will not run out of time***!

➛ *nous aurons tout le temps voulu !*

This slightly extended timeframe takes the bank holiday into account.

➛ *L'échéance a été un peu repoussée et tient compte du jour férié.*

Due to lack of availability for many, Pascale ***has asked that I reschedule*** the demo and, as this time looks convenient for everyone, I hope it will work better.

➛ *m'a demandé de reporter*

Due to conflicts in Christian's and Fred's schedule, we need to reschedule this meeting for next week.

Because of the project ***due dates*** and the holidays, we could not schedule the dinner in December, so the senior team suggested 20 January.
→ *échéances*

I'm looking to set up a ***dry run*** for the closing session on 28 March. Would it be possible for you to change your meeting so we can schedule this session?
→ *galop d'essai*

Please let me know ASAP so I can send out the meeting planner.

May we in that case move the meetings detailed below to Wednesday 8 June?

I'm deleting this series and replacing it with individual occurrences. New calendar appointments to come.
→ *J'annule la périodicité de la réunion et la remplace par des dates spécifiques. Nouvelles demandes de réunions en cours.*

This meeting request ***supersedes*** the previous one.
→ *annule et remplace*

The time of the meeting ***has been amended***/has changed.
→ *L'horaire a été modifié*

"Sorry, ***I told you wrong***. I misread his agenda."
→ *j'ai fait erreur/je vous ai mal renseigné(e)*

I suggest we alter our timings in order to talk to each other by phone.
→ *Pourquoi ne pas modifier nos agendas et trouver un créneau pour un rendez-vous téléphonique ?*

If something comes up and we need to revise the time, I need your mobile number.
→ *S'il y a un empêchement*

The regular Tuesday meeting ***will be held over till*** next week.
➛ *sera reporté à*

"Hello, I was hoping you might have a cancellation today so that you can fit me in."

My preferred choice would be the afternoon slot rather than the morning one.

Please note that the meeting will now be held in room SG 02.
➛ *Veuillez noter qu'à compter d'aujourd'hui, la réunion se tiendra*

Please note the updated room number for the meeting.
➛ *J'attire votre attention sur le nouveau lieu de réunion.*

g) Request for confirmation
Demander confirmation

Please send me a line back confirming receipt of this e-mail.

I hope to hear back from you soon.
➛ *Je vous remercie à l'avance pour votre retour.*

Kindly confirm, ***at your earliest convenience***, whether these dates work for you, in order to facilitate travel arrangements to the meeting site.
➛ *dès que vous serez en mesure de le faire*

h) Confirmation
Confirmer

At your request I am confirming your availability to the head of department.
➛ *À votre demande*

Our preference is for a catered lunch beside the conference room.
➛ *Pour le déjeuner nous privilégions la formule d'un service traiteur*

We have decided on a one-hour lunch break.

➝ *L'option retenue est*

The meeting that showed up on our calendars late yesterday will go ahead in spite of the short notice.

➝ *Bien qu'elle soit de dernière minute, la convocation qui est arrivée hier soir tard est confirmée/la réunion est maintenue.*

i) Accepting an appointment
Accepter un rendez-vous

Ronald ***will be able to attend***.

➝ *sera en mesure de participer.*

You can count him in.

➝ *Vous pouvez compter sur sa participation.*

Although he has a heavy schedule Ronald ***will pop into the meeting***.

➝ *fera un saut à la réunion.*

In spite of his heavy workload, Ronald ***will show his face*** at the meeting

➝ *fera une brève apparition.*

Despite her back to back engagements, she will put in a quick appearance at the meeting.

➝ *Elle a un emploi du temps très serré, mais elle fera une brève apparition à la réunion.*

j) Declining an appointment
Décliner un rendez-vous

Due to "diary constraints" he won't be able to make dinner this evening.

➝ *Ses impératifs/ses contraintes d'agenda ne lui permettront pas de se joindre au dîner*

Theo ***has been roped into a meeting*** on that particular day, so unfortunately he won't be available/won't be free to attend.
➛ *s'est vu imposer/a dû accepter une réunion*

Unfortunately ***Gail is otherwise engaged at that moment/*** that particular time.
➛ *à cette heure-là, Gail est déjà pris*

I have a very bad cold and I'm having trouble talking without coughing this morning. I would prefer to reschedule for tomorrow or Friday when I am in a better condition to talk.

Steve will be in a meeting through till 4 pm, his only availability would be between 4.15 to 5 pm. What do you think?

I think I'll cry off, I don't fancy going to the drinks party after work.
➛ *Je pense me décommander*

k) Declining an invitation
Refuser une invitation

Thanks for extending a lunchtime invitation to Frank. He'd love to join you, but unfortunately he has ***a prior engagement*** on that particular day, however he is available any other day this week.
➛ *contrainte d'emploi du temps/autre engagement*

Would you have another window available?
➛ *Auriez-vous un autre créneau libre ?*

Now is not the best of times. Theo's got a pressing engagement.
➛ *Ce n'est pas le moment idéal.*

l) Duration of an appointment
Durée d'un rendez-vous

I will make sure that Helen ***makes time to review*** and give feedback on the minutes of the meeting.
➛ *ménage le temps de relire/d'étudier*

Because he ***hadn't budgeted enough time for*** the meeting it ended abruptly.

➛ *n'avait pas planifié assez de temps pour*

How much time should I allow for the appraisal? Will it take longer than an hour?

➛ *Combien de temps dois-je prévoir pour l'évaluation/sur combien de temps dois-je tabler ?*

If he's running late, I'll let you know, and we'll plan accordingly/we'll play it by ear/we'll reschedule.

➛ *S'il a pris du retard, je vous tiens au courant et nous agirons en conséquence/nous improviserons/nous reporterons.*

How long can I expect the meeting to last? I need to schedule other appointments.

➛ *Sur combien de temps puis-je tabler pour la réunion ?/ Combien de temps la réunion doit-elle durer ?*

m) Time difference
Décalage horaire

Please note that ***the time slots are given in CET*** (Paris time)/**GMT** (Greenwich Mean Time) and should be adjusted accordingly.

➛ *les horaires correspondent à l'heure d'Europe centrale*

It's currently 5 pm at our end.

➛ *Il est cinq heures actuellement chez nous.*

They've only just arrived from the US, so maybe they are feeling a bit ***whacked and out of synch***.

➛ *« cassés »/vannés et décalés*

Take an hour off the time.

➛ *Reculez vos montres d'une heure.*

Don't forget to add on an hour.

➛ *N'oubliez pas d'ajouter une heure/d'avancer d'une heure.*

Change the time on your watches. France ***is an hour ahead of*** the UK.
➛ *est en avance d'une heure*

You need to ***readjust your watches***.
➛ *remettre vos montres à l'heure.*

Which way are you going with the clock?
➛ *On gagne ou on perd une heure ?*

We are moving forwards/backwards by an hour.
➛ *On avance sa montre/on recule sa montre d'une heure.*

We'll be arriving in Newark at 5.30 pm local time. ***Will we be met at the airport?***
➛ *Y aura-t-il quelqu'un pour nous accueillir à l'aéroport ?*

You need to allow for the time difference. We are 6 hours behind.
➛ *Il vous faut prendre en compte le décalage horaire.*

I've been a day out all week as a result of the overnight flight!
➛ *J'ai été décalé d'un jour toute la semaine*

n) Deadlines
Échéances

Given the short timeframe we have, we need your input by Thursday lunchtime.
➛ *Vu le peu de temps dont nous disposons, vos réponses devront nous parvenir d'ici jeudi midi.*

We have very short timelines to prepare for the meeting.
➛ *L'échéance est courte*

If we could have it wrapped up before the holidays, it would be ideal.
➛ *Si tout était bouclé*

It will be upon us before we know it, so we'd better put our skates on/we'd better pull our socks up/we'd better get our finger out/***we'd better get stuck in***/***we'd better get started***.

➛ *L'échéance arrive à grands pas [...] ne moisissons pas/ mettons-nous y sans tarder.*

When is the latest we can get the manuscript to you?

➛ *Quand au plus tard vous faut-il le manuscrit ?*

When can we get the manuscript to you at the latest?

➛ *Quelle est la date limite à laquelle il vous faut le manuscrit ?*

We can ***let you know where we are at*** and discuss how to proceed shortly.

➛ *vous tenir au courant de là où nous en sommes*

I don't mean to pressurise you, but ***the clock is ticking away and I have a deadline to meet***. I really need the information right now.

➛ *mais l'heure tourne et j'ai des délais à respecter.*

The traffic is flowing, so I don't anticipate any problems. I'd advise Cindy to set off early though, just ***to be on the safe side***.

➛ *pour laisser un peu de marge.*

II. BEING TACTFUL DE LA NUANCE AU TACT

a) Being considerate
Ménager les susceptibilités

Being mindful of your time/being aware of your time, I tied the meeting in with the previous one.

➛ *Soucieuse de ménager votre temps, j'ai fait en sorte que vos deux réunions s'enchaînent.*

Pamela has back to back meetings all of this week, but you have first call on her agenda for next week.

➛ *Pam enchaîne les réunions cette semaine, mais vous avez la priorité/votre rendez-vous sera prioritaire la semaine prochaine.*

It has been duly noted that the introductory meeting is compulsory; however, Ronald has a long-standing engagement that cannot be declined.

➣ *Ronald a pris bonne note du fait que la réunion d'ouverture est obligatoire. Toutefois, il ne peut annuler un rendez vous pris de longue date.*

b) Being flexible
Faire preuve de souplesse

Both are very good for me, ***I'll go with whatever suits the group's needs***.

➣ *Je m'accommoderai de ce qui convient le mieux au groupe.*

I'm pretty flexible; ***I'll go with the majority***.

➣ *j'opterai pour ce que la majorité décide.*

The 25th is currently ***completely clear in my calendar***.

➣ *parfaitement libre dans mon agenda.*

Let's meet ***at a mutually convenient time***.

➣ *à une heure qui convienne à l'un et l'autre/aux uns et aux autres.*

When possible we should accommodate his needs to avoid ***running back and forth*** to the meeting location.

➣ *allées et venues*

Meeting times can be confirmed or altered if necessary.

➣ *Confirmez ou modifiez les horaires de rendez-vous si nécessaire.*

He's pencilled in for later, you can change the time if need be.

➣ *Il est provisoirement inscrit*

Let's settle on that time, and if anything crops up in the meantime, we'll make the necessary arrangements.

➣ *Entendons-nous pour cette date et si entre-temps il y a quelque chose de nouveau, nous ferons les modifications qui s'imposent.*

I'm sure ***we can come to a mutually beneficial arrangement/*** agreement.
➛ *nous pouvons trouver une solution qui nous arrange tous les deux.*

I could conceivably be there on Tuesday, if I juggle my diary.
➛ *Théoriquement, rien ne s'oppose à ce que je vienne, si je jongle avec mon emploi du temps.*

I hope ***my contribution will go part way towards dealing with*** the dilemma.
➛ *que j'aurais apporté ma pierre à l'édifice*

c) Suggesting without being pushy
Proposer sans être tyrannique

I am hoping to review the AED with him ***in advance of*** the meeting on 24 November to ensure his support.
➛ *avant*

I think you might find that an appointment at 11 am will give her little time to recover from her overnight flight.
➛ *À la réflexion lui proposer un rendez-vous à 11 h ne lui permettrait pas de récupérer d'une nuit dans l'avion.*

I intend to ask Joseph for a full hour update rather than the usual weekly half hour. ***Would that be pushing the envelope*** do you think?
➛ *Serait-ce trop demander ?*

You may want to consider rescheduling as this date is not the most suitable for the majority of participants.
➛ *Il serait peut-être souhaitable de reporter*

In my previous message I asked you to decide on a time slot by early afternoon today. ***Personally I'd like to go for*** Wednesday from 12.30 to 3 pm. This could be reduced to one and a half hours if that helps.
➛ *Personnellement, je serais tenté(e) de dire/d'opter pour*

d) Afterthoughts
Revenir sur une erreur ou une maladresse

Immediately after I sent the message below, ***it occurred to me that*** I had forgotten to attach her schedule.
➛ *il m'est venu à l'esprit que*

Reading back through your e-mails, I notice you have not included Helen on your distribution list.
➛ *En relisant vos mails*

I appear to ***have over ordered on*** pre-paid tickets on the Eurostar.
➛ *avoir trop commandé*

For "*Thursday* 8 March" ***read*** "*Friday* 8 March".
➛ *À la place de… lire…*

Having re-read my last mail, it seemed to me that my remark on "…" was unfortunately followed by "….". No offence intended.
➛ *Après relecture de mon dernier mail*

Unfortunately, this information was ***sent in error***. I would recommend the highest discretion.
➛ *envoyée par erreur*

It has been brought to my attention that there was an error in the agenda. Attached is the corrected version.
➛ *Il m'a été signalé que*

e) Suggesting an inconvenient time
Proposer un horaire peu commode

I sincerely ***apologise for running into your lunch time***, but I won't take up much of your time.
➛ *désolé(e) d'empiéter sur l'heure de votre déjeuner*

Would you mind terribly if we changed your 9 o'clock appointment for an appointment at 8.30 am?
➛ *Verriez vous un inconvénient majeur à*

f) Going all out to be available
Se démener pour se rendre disponible

I was willing to ***disrupt my schedule*** tomorrow just to be able to talk to him.

➛ *bousculer mon planning*

I've planned my day to ***make time for*** our weekly update.

➛ *ménager un moment pour*

III. DIFFICULTIES IN SETTING UP AN APPOINTMENT
DIFFICULTÉS DE MISE EN PLACE D'UN RENDEZ-VOUS

I'm sorry; ***I do not have enough rights*** on his calendar to make changes.

➛ *je n'ai pas les accès/les autorisations*

Let's check diaries now and then we'll pick up when I get back from my vacation.

➛ *Faisons un premier point sur nos calendriers et revenons dessus à mon retour de vacances.*

I haven't been able to get the dates to work yet. I hope I'll be able to pull it off. If not, we'll have to look at other dates, I'm afraid.

➛ *Je ne suis pas encore arrivée à faire coïncider toutes les dates. J'espère que ça va être possible.*

I'm still struggling to free up that slot for you.

➛ *C'est la croix et la bannière/c'est la galère pour te libérer ce créneau. Je suis toujours dessus.*

a) Busy schedules
Horaires chargés

As you can imagine, ***our flexibility in choosing a date is very limited since we are having to arrange this meeting around*** our and Rentoval team members' agendas.
➛ *nous avons peu de latitude pour décider d'une date car nous sommes contraints d'organiser cette réunion en fonction de*

I trust you will understand if we are unable to accommodate requests to reschedule the meeting.
➛ *Nous comptons sur votre compréhension si le report de réunion souhaité par les uns et les autres ne peut se faire.*

We are working to arrange the date around our own schedules as well as to suit team members' from Gremkol Ltd.
➛ *Nous faisons en sorte que la date puisse correspondre à/coïncider avec/coller avec nos emplois du temps et convenir à l'équipe de Gremkol Ltd.*

As we are having to ***liaise with*** many individuals who have their own constraints, setting up a date is proving difficult.
➛ *faire le lien entre*

It is proving a juggle fitting everything in to the short timeframe.
➛ *c'est un vrai casse-tête de tout caser/il faut jongler pour tout caser*

Do you think this morning's meeting will be running on time? ***How much time should I allow, before his first meeting*** of the afternoon?
➛ *De combien de temps dispose-t-il avant sa première réunion*

Today is solidly booked for him.
➛ *Aujourd'hui il n'a pas un créneau de libre.*

His desk is piled up with files on this project. I'm not sure he'll be able to make a start on your ***query*** today.
➛ *requête*

Amanda ***has many claims on her timetable***.

➛ *est très sollicitée.*

Time is romping away, I'd better leave our conversation here.

➛ *Le temps passe à toute allure*

A rush job has come in. It has to take priority.

➛ *Un travail urgent*

He has ***back to back meetings*** all day. Let's see what tomorrow looks like.

➛ *Il enchaîne les réunions*

She's just back from sick leave and ***is overwhelmed by the backlog***.

➛ *plie sous le poids des dossiers en retard/à traiter*

I've fallen behind with my work as I spent the whole of yesterday chasing up on the status of pending files.

➛ *J'ai pris du retard dans mon travail ; j'ai passé la journée d'hier à essayer d'établir l'état d'avancement des dossiers en attente.*

We've had ***a rush on*** at the office (dealing with the backlog of orders) and have had to ***put this file on hold***.

➛ *un coup de bourre [...] laisser ce dossier en attente.*

He's drowning in paperwork; unfortunately we'll have to reschedule the meeting.

➛ *Il est en train de se noyer/il croule sous la paperasse*

b) Synchronisation, overlapping
Synchronisation et chevauchements

Even though I have a meeting to go to, ***I still need a full hour*** with Françoise to cover everything.

➛ *il me faut quand même une bonne heure*

My next meeting starts at 9.30 am and I'm already running late ***but I am willing to accommodate Angela's meeting.***

➛ *mais je veux bien trouver un moment dans mon emploi du temps pour la réunion d'Angela/ménager un créneau.*

If I don't hear from you before 3.30 pm, I am going to ***call into my next meeting and assume*** you were able to reschedule my taxi.

➛ *j'entre en réunion et pars du principe que*

The meeting falls at the same time as my year end review, so it needs to be rescheduled.

➛ *La réunion tombe au même moment que*

This is my B2B time commitment, I'm not available.

➛ *Ceci est le créneau habituellement réservé à/affecté à ma réunion B2B*

I am still trying to ***pull everything together***, would Thursday work for you to take a look at the final ***draft***?

➛ *rassembler toutes les données [...] avant projet ?*

Assuming Paul gets a taxi he still won't be able to get here on time for a 2.30 start this afternoon! ***Let's think along other lines.***

➛ *Il va falloir trouver autre chose.*

c) Apologies for a late reply
Répondre en retard et s'en excuser

I am sorry I did not get back to you earlier but I wanted to discuss this with a couple of managers before I give you my final answer.

➛ *Je suis désolé(e) de n'être pas revenu(e) vers vous plus tôt/ de ne pas avoir repris contact*

Your mail came through late last night. I'm sorry; I've only just picked it up.

➛ *Votre courriel est arrivé tard hier soir. Désolé(e) je viens à peine de l'ouvrir.*

I must have overlooked your mail. Profuse apologies. I'll get on to it straight away.

➛ *Sans doute n'ai-je pas vu votre courriel. Je suis confus(e). Je m'y attelle tout de suite.*

IV. AVAILABILITY LES DISPONIBILITÉS DES UNS ET DES AUTRES

I'm sorry ***he's tied up in a meeting***. Would you like him to call you back?

➛ *il est retenu par une réunion.*

Ram would like to discuss the matter with you ***fairly rapidly***. Please could you confirm your availability?

➛ *relativement vite.*

He is ***available for a two-day meeting on either side of these weeks.*** Which would you prefer?

➛ *disponible pour un meeting de deux jours soit avant soit après les semaines en question.*

Please let us know if you would like to send a representative ***if you are unable to attend***?

➛ *si vous êtes dans l'impossibilité de participer*

I will be ***on call*** if there's an emergency and you need to get hold of me.

➛ *d'astreinte*

He has a prior engagement which can be cancelled if necessary.

➛ *Il est déjà pris*

I have ***a gap in my diary on Monday between 2 and 3 pm***. Would that suit?

➛ *un creux/un trou dans mon emploi du temps lundi entre 14 heures et 15 heures.*

Let me take a look, ***I may have the odd space in my diary***.

➛ *il se peut que je trouve un moment libre on ne sait jamais.*

I'm sorry, ***he's unavoidably detained***. He's running half an hour late.

➛ *il est retenu/il a un empêchement, pour des raisons indépendantes de sa volonté.*

Time

Autour du temps

I. DEADLINES ÉCHÉANCES

a) Avant

Be sure to send it in advance of the 24th.
➛ *Veillez à l'envoyer avant le 24.*

Just give me 15 minutes' warning, will you?
➛ *Pensez à me prévenir un quart d'heure à l'avance.*

We're a few minutes shy of starting.
➛ *Il nous reste quelques minutes avant de commencer.*

Sorry we didn't call ahead.
➛ *Désolé de ne pas avoir téléphoné à l'avance.*

It will be another half hour yet.
➛ *Ce ne sera pas avant une demi-heure.*

The newsletter is due on one side or the other of the Christmas holidays.
➛ *Le journal interne devrait paraître juste avant ou juste après les congés de Noël.*

b) Délais

We're only a month away from launching the new products.
➛ *Le lancement des nouveaux produits est dans à peine un mois.*

The meeting is just an hour and a half away.
➛ *La réunion est dans à peine une heure et demie.*

The timeline we have laid out (three hours) is sufficient.
➛ *L'échéance que nous avons prévue (trois heures) est suffisante.*

c) Prévoir

It was timed to begin at 3.30 pm.
→ *C'était programmé pour/cela devait commencer à/ c'était prévu pour commencer à 15 h 30.*

It's better to allow a bit of extra time.
→ *Mieux vaut prévoir large.*

I'm a little behind where I intended to be at this time.
→ *J'ai un peu de retard par rapport à ce que j'avais prévu/ à l'objectif que je m'étais fixé.*

d) Prochain

I'll be in touch in the not too distant future.
→ *Je vous recontacte prochainement, sous peu*

In the next quarter of an hour.
→ *Dans les prochaines quinze minutes.*

e) Retard

We overshot the time by 10 minutes (= we overran by 10 minutes).
→ *Nous avons pris 10 minutes de retard.*

I left it a bit late to ring you.
→ *J'ai un peu tardé à vous appeler.*

I'm annoyed as I've put myself at least two hours behind the schedule I'd set myself.
→ *Je suis contrarié(e) de m'être mis(e) en retard de deux heures par rapport au programme que je m'étais fixé.*

II. TIMEFRAME CRÉNEAUX HORAIRES

a) Créneau

Could you text at some point between those times?
➛ *Trouverez-vous un moment dans ce créneau là pour envoyer un SMS ?*

I will look out for a slot.
➛ *Dès que j'entrevois un créneau, je vous tiens au courant.*

b) Heure

It's coming up to 10 o'clock.
➛ *Il est presque dix heures/On approche des 10 heures.*

At this time of the day.
➛ *À cette heure de la journée.*

He was here this morning, but I couldn't put a time to it.
➛ *Il est passé ce matin, mais je ne pourrais pas vous dire à quelle heure/quand exactement.*

That's just one hour from now.
➛ *Dans à peine une heure.*

We must be there on the half hour, but I'll get in at 10.20 am.
➛ *On doit y être à la demie, mais j'y serai à 10 h 20.*

In the last half (an) hour.
➛ *Pendant les trente dernières minutes.*

We officially work one hour less as we have an early 4 pm finish on a Friday.
➛ *Officiellement, le vendredi on termine de bonne heure.*

The launching ran on until 1 pm.
➛ *Le lancement a duré jusqu'à 13 heures.*

c) Heures

Sorry I'm late; I'll make up the time.
➛ *Désolé(e) d'être en retard. Je rattraperai mes heures.*

Sort it out on your time!
➛ *Prenez sur vos heures pour régler le problème.*

We were still editing to a few hours before transmission.
➛ *À quelques heures de la transmission, nous en étions toujours à la phase de montage.*

In two hours flat.
➛ *En deux heures chrono/deux heures pile.*

d) Horaires

The start and finish time of the meeting.
➛ *Les horaires de la réunion.*

Please note the start time of the meeting has altered slightly by half an hour.
➛ *Veuillez noter le léger changement d'horaire de la réunion qui commencera une demi-heure plus tôt.*

I'm glad to be able to leave at our usual Friday early finishing time of 4 pm!
➛ *Je suis ravi de profiter des horaires du vendredi et de partir à 16 heures !*

I hope your RER delay will not be disastrous to your timing.
➛ *J'espère que le retard dans le RER ne va pas trop bousculer vos horaires.*

e) Moment

I could try stealing a few minutes out of the day (to call the bank).
➛ *J'essaierai de trouver un petit moment dans la journée (pour appeler la banque).*

The problem was the timing (someone showing up unexpectedly or too early).
➛ *Cela ne tombait pas au bon moment/n'était pas opportun.*

Could you free up the time to come with me?
➛ *Pourriez-vous vous libérer pour m'accompagner/pourriez-vous ménager un moment ?*

f) Pause

I'm on my lunch break
➛ *Je suis en pause déjeuner.*

g) Temps

We're almost at the end of our time now, it's 10 o'clock (meeting).
➛ *Il sera bientôt temps de clôturer cette réunion.*

(The) Time allowed for the speech.
➛ *Le temps imparti/autorisé/prévu pour le discours.*

We are well within our time limit.
➛ *Nous sommes largement dans les temps/nous ne sommes pas en retard.*

In nothing flat.
➛ *En deux temps trois mouvements.*

The greatest Frenchman of all time.
➛ *Le Français le plus illustre de l'Histoire/de tous les temps.*

It's all going to time.
➛ *Nous sommes dans les temps.*

The turnaround time of an order.
➛ *Le temps d'exécution d'une commande.*

Tasks become more urgent with the passing of time.
➛ *Quand on laisse le temps passer, on se retrouve à travailler dans l'urgence.*

How are we doing for time?
➢ *Qu'est-ce que ça donne au niveau du temps ?/Sommes-nous dans les temps ?*

It took up a large part of the day, but there was still time to fit in a one-to-one with Simon.
➢ *Cela a monopolisé pratiquement toute la journée, mais il restait encore un peu de temps pour un entretien individuel avec Simon.*

We'll deal with the refinements in due course.
➢ *Nous fignolerons les détails en temps utile.*

What sort of timeframe would you attach to it?/are we looking at?
➢ *À combien estimez-vous le temps nécessaire ?*

Someone on duty at all times.
➢ *Quelqu'un de garde en permanence/tout le temps.*

III. COORDINATING COORDINATION

a) Décaler

Change the meeting by one day.
➢ *Décaler la réunion d'une journée.*

Because your timing goes completely out of the window.
➢ *Car toute la synchronisation tombe à l'eau/tout est décalé.*

You'll have to shift the meeting time back by an hour and a half.
➢ *Il te faudra décaler/avancer l'heure de ton rendez-vous d'une heure et demie.*

His visit might throw the usual timings.
➢ *Sa visite risque de décaler les horaires habituels.*

b) Fois

The number of people allowed in at any one time.
➢ *Le maximum de personnes autorisées en une seule fois/ d'un seul coup/à chaque fois.*

c) Marge

You might be cutting it fine (train connection).
➛ *C'est peut-être prévoir un peu juste/ça ne vous laisse pas beaucoup de marge.*

d) Ponctuel

Let's do things as and when.
➛ *Faisons les choses ponctuellement/quand l'occasion se présentera.*

To be punctual.
➛ *Être ponctuel (à un rendez-vous).*

To be a good time keeper.
➛ *Être ponctuel (trait de caractère).*

You're right on time.
➛ *Vous êtes parfaitement à l'heure/vous êtes ponctuel, dites moi !*

e) Synchronisation

That's good timing!
➛ *Bonne synchronisation !*
➛ *Vous arrivez juste bien !*

We must get the timing right (train connection/taxi ride to the airport).
➛ *Il faut s'assurer que les horaires correspondent/que la synchronisation sera bonne (correspondance de train/taxi).*

You timed that well; I was just about to give you a call!
➛ *Tu tombes à point, j'allais justement t'appeler !*

f) Tôt

Not before time!
➛ *Ce n'est pas trop tôt/Enfin !*

I had a very early start and late finish today.
➛ *J'ai commencé très tôt ce matin et je suis parti(e) tard le soir.*

IV. MISCELLANEOUS AUTRES

There will be times for us to talk further.
➛ *Nous trouverons des occasions de parler plus à loisir.*

It will cut the journey time by half.
➛ *Cela réduira le voyage de moitié.*

He spent the intervening time checking his missed calls.
➛ *Entre les deux, il a passé son temps à vérifier ses appels manqués.*

Then the next day is on you before you have time to turn around.
➛ *Et sans vous en apercevoir, vous êtes déjà au lendemain/la journée est passée.*

You made good time, I thought you'd be caught up in the traffic jams.
➛ *Tu n'as pas été long/tu as fait vite pour venir/tu n'as pas traîné/tu as bien roulé, je pensais que tu serais pris dans les embouteillages.*

Telephone

Téléphone

I. LANDLINE FIXES

I am calling the travel agency ***as we speak***.
➛ *à l'instant même.*

Let me stand by while you're sending me the mail, then we can look at it together.
➛ *Je reste en ligne pendant que tu me fais suivre le document*

He's not picking up; he must be on his way to the meeting.
➛ *Il ne décroche pas*

I'm calling her; ***it's ringing out***.
➛ *ça sonne dans le vide.*

The line automatically kicks over to the other line.
➛ *L'appel est automatiquement transféré sur l'autre ligne.*

The line broke down, so I had to redial the number/renew my call.
➛ *Nous avons été coupés*

Reception is bad, ***the line is crackly***.
➛ *il y a de la friture sur la ligne.*

You're breaking up.
➛ *Je ne vous capte plus.*

The line sounds broken, I'll call you back.
➛ *La ligne est mauvaise, je rappelle.*

That was ***a very hiccupy phone call***, the line kept breaking up.
➛ *un appel très mouvementé*

Local calling is ok, but when I call abroad the line is dead.
➛ *Aucune difficulté pour appeler localement, mais pour l'étranger il n'y a pas de tonalité.*

You've gone faint now, can you speak up?
➛ *Ta voix est lointaine/je t'entends de moins en moins bien*

We'll hook up tomorrow, call me at 10 o'clock.
➛ *Nous reprendrons contact*

I'm hooked up again; my phone was out of order all morning!
➛ *Je suis de nouveau joignable*

I'm contactable again.
➛ *Je suis de nouveau joignable.*

Sorry I was a bit late getting back to you, but *I was* ***away from my phone***.
➛ *je n'étais pas à proximité de mon téléphone.*

Let me repeat that back to you and check I've got the correct address.
➛ *Je répète et vérifie que j'ai bien noté l'adresse.*

Contact me on that number, that's the phone I'll be using.
➛ *Appelez-moi à ce numéro*

He wants me to ***install a ringtone*** on his mobile phone. How about I downloaded "Ha,Ha,Ha,Ha,Ha, funny Ha"?!
➛ *installer une sonnerie*

On the other end of the phone.
➛ *À l'autre bout du fil.*

I can hear you well ***at my end***, what about you?
➛ *de mon côté*

As mentioned previously over the phone, the post office is still on strike/we are still encountering problems with the postal service.
➛ *Comme nous l'avons déjà évoqué au téléphone*

Due to the high volume of calls, my call couldn't be taken. I'll have to try again later.
➛ *En raison du grand nombre d'appels*

I got walked in on, so I cut my call short/I ended my call.
➣ *Quelqu'un est entré et j'ai dû raccrocher.*

I'll put a call in to the boss and ask if he's available to have lunch with you.
➣ *Je vais essayer de joindre le patron*

One well-placed call can save us the rigmarole of having to go through the official channels, so let's call the manager directly.
➣ *Mieux vaut bien cibler notre appel, cela nous évitera de passer par des formalités sans fin/mieux vaut s'adresser au bon Dieu qu'à ses saints.*

Bear with me, I'm on hold with my American counterpart.
➣ *Veuillez patienter, on m'a mis(e) en attente*

Can you give me a call back when you get this?
➣ *Peux-tu me rappeler quand tu reçois ce message ?*

I'm having my calls re-routed.
➣ *Je fais suivre mes appels.*

"***I'm sorry to trouble you.*** I know Amanda is in a meeting right now, could she be interrupted?"
➣ *Désolé de vous déranger.*

I'm just off the phone to her, and I've got the answer I was waiting for.
➣ *Je viens à peine de l'avoir au téléphone*

I know not to pick up when they call, as their number shows up on my phone.
➣ *Quand c'est leur numéro qui s'affiche, je me garde bien de décrocher.*

Can't you "Instant Message" your boss ***while she's on her call***?
➣ *pendant qu'elle a son rendez-vous téléphonique ?*

I've got another call coming through, we need to wind up this call.
➣ *J'ai un autre appel, il va falloir raccrocher.*

I'll sign off now; talk to you later.
➣ *Je raccroche, à plus tard.*

Sorry if I have to cut you off at some point, but I'm expecting the computer technician any minute.

➛ *Excusez-moi si je dois vous interrompre à un moment donné*

II. TELECONFERENCES TÉLÉCONFÉRENCES

We're all smiling in agreement here...

➛ *Mines ravies de notre côté, pas l'ombre d'une objection...*

The majority seem to be nodding in agreement to your suggestion, it sounds like a good idea.

➛ *Si j'en crois les hochements de tête, pratiquement tout le monde est d'accord. L'idée est bonne.*

I can see lots of worried faces round the table; ***can you expand on that a little more***?

➛ *pouvez-vous développer un peu/en dire davantage ?*

A few people are raising their eyebrows. Not everyone is convinced by the looks of it.

➛ *Il y a quelques froncements de sourcils autour de la table. Apparemment, tout le monde n'est pas convaincu.*

My assistant has just popped in to relay a message to me, ***can you just hold it there a minute***?

➛ *on peut s'interrompre un instant ?*

Bear with us while Andrew goes and gets the document off the printer.

➛ *Vous allez devoir patienter un peu*

Sorry, we lost you there for a minute, can you hear us ok?

➛ *Désolé, il y a eu un blanc pendant une minute*

We just had a bit of a commotion –someone double booked the room and stormed in, but it is all settled now/but we're back on track now.

➛ *Excusez le remue-ménage ; en fait, notre salle avait été réservée par un autre collègue et quelqu'un vient de faire irruption tout à coup*

Sorry can you just hold on for a minute, ***I can hear raised voices just outside*** which is very off-putting. I'll be right back/won't be a sec/give me a minute.
➛ *il y a des gens qui parlent fort dans le couloir*

As soon as ***the late comers*** have settled down, we can start.
➛ *les retardataires*

We were ***placed on music hold***, and it took forever to be connected.
➛ *mis en attente musicale*

As we had difficulty getting through, ***we double-checked the dial-in number*** to be sure it was correct.
➛ *nous avons revérifié le numéro d'accès à la conférence*

For the final round of discussions I suggest we invite Pete to ***call in on our weekly audio-conference***.
➛ *participer/se connecter à notre conférence hebdomadaire.*

Meeting ***face to face*** isn't an option. ***How about we host a Web meeting***?
➛ *face à face [...] Et si nous organisions un Web meeting ?*

III. MOBILES PORTABLES

I hope ***my credit extends as far as the transmission of this message***.
➛ *que j'aurai assez de crédit pour t'envoyer ce message/pour que mon message parte.*

I'm getting low on battery, but think it will last out.
➛ *Ma batterie faiblit, mais ça devrait être suffisant.*

I need to buy a voucher to top up.
➛ *Il faut que je m'achète une recharge.*

I'm not sure my text has transmitted.
➛ *Je ne suis pas sûr que mon SMS soit parti.*

Would you please make sure your phones are in silent mode, ***there's nothing worse than a phone going off*** in the middle of a presentation.

➛ *rien de pire qu'un téléphone qui se met à sonner*

Out of the office messages

Messages en absence

I. ELECTRONIC MAIL COURRIER ÉLECTRONIQUE

I will be out of the office from February, 22-24 inclusive.

I will be out of the office from Friday 8 October and will return on Monday 18 October. During this time I will only have intermittent access to e-mail.

I'm currently away from my desk or on the other line. For urgent matters, please contact Sophie D. on 4334.

I will respond to your e-mail tomorrow when I am back at my desk and out of training.

Claire is off site today, but she will be able to access your calls on her mobile phone.

I will be off site on Tuesday 15 February and I anticipate being back on Wednesday.

I am currently unavailable. Should you require assistance, please contact Kevin P. on 4337.

I'm sorry I'm currently unavailable; you can reach me as of Tuesday 7 February.

II. RECORDED MESSAGES RÉPONDEURS

I'm sorry I can't take your call at the moment, but leave me a message and I'll get back to you as soon as I can.

This is Bill Burton's office. I'm not available right now, but if you leave your number and the reason for your call I'll get back to you.

Travelling

Voyages

I. TRAVEL ARRANGEMENTS ORGANISER DES DÉPLACEMENTS

a) Organising: thinking ahead
Anticiper

I don't expect any problems but wanted to provide this schedule for you just in case one should arise/***to be on the safe side***.

➛ *par précaution.*

Forward to Catherine any itineraries that have been set up for Amanda.

➛ *Transmettez à*

The itinerary in its current state shows that Amanda will be staying three nights in Paris, but this is ***liable to change***.

➛ *susceptible de changer.*

I spoke to our travel agency ***to get estimated pricing*** for flights but obviously prices will increase if I don't book shortly.

➛ *pour avoir un ordre d'idées du prix*

Could you try and ***firm up the plans*** so I can book the flight?

➛ *confirmer les dispositions prises*

Please, ***hold the train booking*** **until** Tom has decided how he wants to travel. I have a feeling he might want to take the plane.

➛ *veuillez mettre une option sur ce billet de train jusqu'à ce que*

I must remember that Veronica needs extra ***leg room*** when I book her airline tickets.

➛ *dégagement pour les jambes*

I'm hoping to ***take a short side-trip*** over to Paris/making a detour via Paris/make a short stopover in Paris. Could you check out hotel possibilities for me?

➛ *un intermède/visite touristique*

If I understand correctly, ***it is a 20 to 25 minute train ride*** from Newark Airport to New York Penn station.

➛ *le trajet dure 20 à 25 minutes*

Is the train from the airport to New York Penn direct? If not, ***which stations does it call at***?

➛ *quelles gares le train dessert-il ?*

Would Ian have to change trains at some point?/Somewhere along the line?

➛ *Y aurait-il un changement pour Ian*

Once it has called at Newark Penn ***does the train make further stops*** before its final destination?/does it then go on directly to New York Penn?/does it stop again before reaching New York Penn?

➛ *le train s'arrête-t-il à d'autres gares*

How much time should be allowed for the journey?

➛ *Combien de temps faut-il compter/prévoir*

If he decides to change ***the pick-up location of the hire car,*** we would need advance notice to accommodate this change.

➛ *le lieu de la prise en charge du véhicule de location*

When I checked the online booking site, ***there was no mention of departures from*** Newark Penn station to Boston South, only New York Penn.

➛ *on ne mentionnait nulle part de départs à partir de/il n'y avait aucune référence à un départ de*

For all travel outside North America ***a request must be submitted and approved by the VP***.

➛ *une demande doit être soumise au Vice Président et validée par lui.*

My visa ran out ages ago. What's the time frame for getting a new one?
➛ *Mon visa est périmé depuis longtemps.*

I was able to get a room in a first-rate hotel in Paris for the entire time and ***remain within the company's travel policy, budget wise***.
➛ *n'ai pas dépassé le budget voyage en vigueur dans la société.*

A lot of travellers ***are currently on a waiting list*** for rooms in Lyon at this time of year. The annual trade show attracts thousands of visitors.
➛ *sont actuellement sur liste d'attente*

b) Organising: adjustments
Régler les points de détail

Please note per your request through Shawn Lawrence that ***I have adjusted the car service pick-up time to 3 pm instead of 4 pm***.
➛ *j'ai avancé à 15 heures le service de transport au lieu des 16 heures initiales.*

I have got ***the train times*** that you requested for your return trip with Eurostar. We can now reschedule it.
➛ *les horaires de trains*

Susannah's travel arrangements are finalised. ***Everything checks out, there are no loose ends.***
➛ *Tout est bon, on a tout bouclé.*

You can count on us to ***meet her off the 11:45 Eurostar***.
➛ *la retrouver à l'arrivée de l'Eurostar de 11 h 45.*

c) Transport and timing (adverse weather conditions or not)
Transport et synchronisation (intempéries ou non)

Car service reservations to and from the airport should be made ***in good time***/well ahead of departure.

➛ *suffisamment à l'avance.*

Our regular taxi driver will collect Ian the following day and ***take him back to the airport***.

➛ *viendra le rechercher pour le conduire à l'aéroport.*

The driver will get you there well in advance to ***allow for sometimes lengthy check-ins, passport control and security clearance.***

➛ *avoir une marge pour les enregistrements souvent interminables, contrôles de passeport et formalités de sécurité.*

The possible dates for a short stopover in Paris are Tuesday 5 and Thursday 7 March.

In relation to taxi transfers, ***I will make enquiries into booking your ground transportation once*** I have your flight details.

➛ *je me renseignerai sur la réservation des transferts sur place*

You should ***allow sufficient time to claim your luggage***, which can be somewhat slow at times.

➛ *prévoir une certaine marge pour récupérer les bagages*

I have already informed Daserole Livery and they'll be keeping tabs on your re-scheduled arrival time.

➛ *J'en ai informé la société Daserole et ils assureront votre suivi en fonction du nouvel horaire.*

Be prepared to ***sit in traffic*** on the ring road no matter what time you arrive.

➛ *être bloqué au volant/coincé dans un embouteillage*

The traffic is crawling along/at a standstill/chock-a-block/ bumper to bumper. Don't wait for me, go ahead with the meeting.

➛ *On roule au pas – la circulation est bloquée – les routes sont saturées – les voitures sont à touche-touche.*

The Eurostar has been thrown into chaos yet again due to adverse weather conditions.

➛ *L'Eurostar est plongé dans la confusion la plus totale*

The train left 30 minutes behind time. When I arrived at the Gare du Nord, I'd missed my RER connection.

➛ *Le train est parti avec 30 minutes de retard.*

Although the office is not far from the station, you will have to ***contend with 10 miles of hair-pin bends***. This will slow you down considerably.

➛ *négocier une bonne quinzaine de kilomètres en épingle à cheveux.*

If by any chance you end up missing the turn, ***you'll overshoot into the next village***. Just turn around and make your way back.

➛ *vous êtes bon pour aller/vous devrez aller jusqu'au village suivant.*

Motorists are going nowhere fast this morning due to heavy fog. It might be advisable to work from home until it lifts.

➛ *Les automobilistes n'avancent guère/sont ralentis*

I'd think twice about travelling that week-end. It is when ***the great Xmas getaway*** begins.

➛ *les grands départs de Noël*

I've just heard ***there's lots of standing water on minor roads***. It would be best if you kept to the motorway for as long as possible.

➛ *certaines routes secondaires sont partiellement inondées*

CO #57 at 9:55 am is sold out on the 22nd, would you like me to put you on the waiting list?

➛ *il n'y a plus de place sur le vol CO #57 de 9 h 55*

We got the train ***without a minute to spare***/by the skin of our teeth.
➛ *de justesse.*

They arrived ***a full two hours before they were due***.
➛ *deux bonnes heures avant l'heure prévue.*

I will try to get into Paris ***before the transport system collapses***. Heavy snow is causing major problems.
➛ *avant que les transports ne soient complètement paralysés.*

II. MEETING AND GREETING ACCUEIL ET TRANSFERTS

a) Signage
Panneaux nominatifs

There will be ***a sign with Tom's name on*** that will be held by the Daserole driver.
➛ *pancarte au nom de Tom*

After Tom has collected his luggage, passed through customs and come through the sliding doors, ***he will be met by a chauffeur***.
➛ *un chauffeur l'attendra.*

I made arrangements for Ann to be picked up from the airport at 3 pm and be taken to the Gremkol office.
➛ *j'ai prévu que quelqu'un vienne chercher Ann*

For your convenience, we have asked the Rosedale driver to have a sign with your name for easy identification. As soon as you come through the door after getting your luggage, the driver ***will be in the arrival area holding the sign***.
➛ *vous attendra dans le hall des arrivées avec une pancarte.*

Someone will be at the airport ***to meet and greet you.***
➛ *pour assurer votre accueil*

b) Arrival as of landing: procedures to follow (luggage, customs, transport and hotels)

Formalités à l'arrivée

It's advisable to get a trolley ***before heading to the carrousel*** to pick up your luggage.

➛ *avant de vous diriger vers le tapis roulant*

Be prepared to wait a while ***before your suitcase comes on to the carrousel***.

➛ *avant que votre valise n'arrive sur le tapis roulant.*

Once Tom arrives at the airport, ***how much further does he have to walk to the check-in desk***?

➛ *il y a encore long à marcher jusqu'à la zone d'enregistrement ?*

Where are you aiming for, the north of Paris or the centre?

➛ *Où voulez vous vous rendre*

The two buildings are ***only a few minutes apart***; you can easily walk back and forth.

➛ *à quelques minutes l'un de l'autre*

What time does your train get in on Thursday?

➛ *À quelle heure votre train arrive-t-il ?*

Do you intend staying the night? Shall I make a reservation for you?

➛ *Pensez-vous rester la nuit ?*

Within 5 minutes of getting off the train you can be at your desk, the office is so close to the station.

➛ *Vous sortez du train et cinq minutes plus tard vous êtes à votre bureau*

After a quick freshen up I'll be ready for the meeting.

➛ *Quand je me serai rendu(e) plus présentable*

Round the corner, straight on up until you come to the metro station.
➛ *Tournez au coin de la rue et prenez la côte*

Just up/down the road from our office.
➛ *À quelques pas de/pas loin de*

I live ***round the corner from work***.
➛ *à deux pas de mon travail.*

Extra shuttle services can be laid on at the last minute (during unexpectedly busy times or strikes).
➛ *Des navettes supplémentaires peuvent être mises à disposition*

You will find ***your rental/hire car*** at parking bay n° 15.
➛ *votre voiture de location*

Park the car and ***feed the meter***.
➛ *mettez de l'argent dans l'horodateur.*

It is no distance at all.
➛ *Ce n'est pas loin du tout.*

The company car is going to be ***parked up*** for a while.
➛ *immobilisée*

Your car's gone into the garage for repair/it is being serviced. ***Your best bet*** would be to take a taxi.
➛ *Le mieux*

Taxis are few and far between late at night/taxis are thin on the ground, so it might be a good idea to book now.
➛ *Les taxis se font rares le soir tard*

c) Security clearance on business premises
Démarches de sécurité dans l'enceinte de l'entreprise

Upon your arrival at the Toronto site, ***the car will make a stop*** at Building 4. It will then proceed to Building 83 where the meeting is to be held.
➛ *votre taxi effectuera un arrêt*

Security will sign you in; there'll be no need for you to get out of the car.
➛ *Les agents de sécurité vous enregistreront*

We have ***locked storage*** on our premises where you can leave your luggage if necessary.
➛ *un lieu de dépôt sécurisé pour les bagages*

Just in case, ***I'll take care of clearance***. However, this may not be necessary as some associates from Paris have valid US badges.
➛ *je me charge des autorisations d'entrée*

III. VISITORS' OFFICES BUREAUX DE PASSAGE

Could you make sure I have ***a workspace*** on Monday morning and throughout the rest of the week?
➛ *un endroit où m'installer pour travailler*

The VTC Room is already booked, in order to avoid any conflict ***we would be happy to withdraw our reservation***.
➛ *nous serions tout à fait disposés à annuler notre réservation.*

If you can find a smaller office for Stephanie, Linda and I would be happy to share her current office ***which could easily accommodate the two of us*** all day Thursday for a meeting.
➛ *qui serait suffisamment grand pour toutes les deux/pourrait aisément nous loger*

The "minute-meeting" rooms are fitted out with international telephone lines. On an experimental basis and ***in order to avoid double bookings***, please fill in the booking form on each door (date, time, user's name).

➛ *pour éviter une réservation en double*

Seminars
Séminaires

I. ORGANISING ORGANISATION ET PRÉPARATIFS

a) Transportation
Transports

For those team members joining us from out of town or from abroad, details on hotel accommodation and ***directions to the meeting location will be sent out via a separate e-mail*** along with an agenda.

➤ *le plan d'accès au lieu de la réunion sera communiqué dans un mail séparé*

Delegates wishing to use this bus service should contact reception.

➤ *Les participants/congressistes*

The conference hall is situated ***across the roundabout from the station***.

➤ *de l'autre côté du rond point en sortant de la gare.*

We regret that ***we are unable to offer alternative collecting times***.

➤ *aucun service de navette ne sera assuré en dehors des horaires indiqués.*

For the smooth running of transport to our kick-off meeting please consult the lists posted on the doors next to reception, ***advising which vehicle you'll be sharing*** to get to our destination.

➤ *Afin que le transfert vers le lieu de notre réunion de lancement se déroule dans les meilleures conditions/afin de faciliter le transfert […] indiquant le véhicule de votre choix*

Should you require a lift to the seminar, please ***sign up*** on one of the four lists available at reception/posted on the meeting room doors.
➛ *inscrivez-vous*

Each list shows a specific departure time.
➛ *Chaque liste correspond à une heure de départ différente.*

A notice will be posted up for those who wish to put their names down.
➛ *Vous pourrez inscrire votre nom sur l'affiche réservée à cet effet.*

b) List of participants and badges
Liste des participants et badges

Participants who confirmed attendance are invited to arrive at the reception desk well in advance of the 9 am conference opening time ***to claim their security badges***.
➛ *pour retirer leurs badges.*

You are invited to sign in upon arrival at the reception desk.
➛ *Vous êtes invité à vous enregistrer à l'accueil dès votre arrivée.*

She ***is standing in for someone who's pulled out at the last minute***. I can use a spare badge and write her name on it.
➛ *remplace quelqu'un qui s'est désisté au dernier moment.*

I can use a blank card and print it out/***write out a makeshift badge***, but I'm afraid it will not include the logo and will not look as professional.
➛ *établir un badge provisoire à la main*

Currently there are no vacancies for February. However, ***we'll be running another course*** on 17 March – would you like to sign up?
➛ *nous organiserons une autre formation*

c) Colour scheme, freebies and goody bags
Thème couleur, cadeaux promotionnels, mercatique

The colour scheme is keyed to brown.

➛ *Les coloris s'harmonisent autour du brun.*

With the hotel manager ***we have arranged for freebies to be laid out*** on the table in each hotel room. Participants will find them on arrival.

➛ *nous sommes convenus de disposer des petits cadeaux de bienvenue*

The freebies ***will be stylishly presented in small bags*** and there'll be one for each participant.

➛ *seront élégamment présentés dans des petits sacs*

The ***freebies will be handed out* to** participants as they come in.

➛ *Les petits cadeaux de bienvenue/cadeaux d'accueil seront distribués*

II. THE INS AND OUTS OF THE DAY'S AGENDA
AUTOUR DE L'ORDRE DU JOUR

May we take this opportunity to remind participants that ***we'll be wrapping up the meeting at 4 o'clock sharp***/on the dot?

➛ *nous terminerons notre réunion à 4 heures précises*

This agenda item will have to be deferred until further notice.

➛ *Ce point d'ordre du jour va devoir être reporté jusqu'à nouvel ordre.*

These questions needn't be dealt with immediately. They ***can stand over until our next meeting***.

➛ *peuvent rester en suspens/jusqu'à/attendre la prochaine réunion.*

We need to ***keep the meeting moving on schedule and on topic***, otherwise, we'll end up running late.

➛ *nous en tenir à l'horaire et éviter les digressions*

The delegates are invited to adjourn to the bar where drinks will be served.

➣ *Les congressistes sont invités à passer au bar*

A short comfort break is called for, let's stop there and make a beeline for the coffee machine.

➣ *Une courte pause biologique/une courte pause réparatrice s'impose*

I'm in the middle of tidying up my reports in view of the upcoming conference.

➣ *Compte tenu de la prochaine conférence, j'ai entrepris de mettre de l'ordre dans mes rapports.*

Each session is designed to build upon the previous one, so I strongly encourage attendance at all meetings.

➣ *L'idée est de faire en sorte que chaque séance soit basée sur la précédente*

I have arranged the weekend to leave you with free time to explore our remarkable outdoor setting/the vicinity/the beautiful surroundings.

➣ *J'ai fait en sorte de ménager des plages de liberté qui vous permettront d'explorer les environs splendides.*

We will run through the session during lunch in order to save time/ to economise on your precious time. Please be sure to have your speaker notes prepared for this meeting.

➣ *Nous préparerons la séance au cours d'un déjeuner de travail*

From the company we would aim to have Peter, Christophe and myself participating.

➣ *Comme représentants de notre société, nous proposons Peter, Christophe et moi-même.*

The last item has been removed from the agenda/dropped from the agenda.

➣ *Ce dernier point a été retiré de l'ordre du jour.*

We'll have to ***bump these items off the agenda***/push them off the agenda due to a lack of time.
➛ *éliminer ces points/les rayer de l'ordre du jour*

Hope the training sessions ***are going along well***.
➛ *se déroulent bien.*

Dotted throughout the day, there will be a series of product demos/short informative films/short sessions on ways in which to relax.
➛ *Ponctuant la journée*

Sessions ***outside these core hours*** will be devoted to workshops on specific areas of concern.
➛ *en dehors des réunions clé/hors des séances plénières*

During non-core hours participants will be able to take advantage of the latest product demos.
➛ *En dehors des réunions plénières*

The item ***was pushed to the end*** of the agenda.
➛ *est passé en dernière position*

If you start to overrun the timetable, bring the discussion back to the agenda and get back on track.
➛ *Si vous commencez à prendre du retard, ramenez la discussion sur l'ordre du jour et reprenez le fil.*

Ensure the meeting is ***focused and productive***.
➛ *bien centré sur/ne dévie pas du sujet et donne lieu à de riches discussions.*

III. CONFERENCE MATERIAL
SÉLECTIONNER LES SUJETS ET LEURS QUESTIONS

We will also have the opportunity to ***submit questions via text*** during the meeting.
➛ *soumettre des questions par SMS*

We would like to provide a few starting points for the meeting's agenda, and ***request additional input or suggestions from yourselves***.

→ *comptons sur vos propres contributions et suggestions.*

The speech must ***be pitched at the right level*** so that everyone gets the message.

→ *adapté à l'auditoire*

Those with the least knowledge should not feel out of their depth.

→ *Il ne faut pas que les moins avertis se sentent dépassés.*

Should you wish to submit a topic or a question for discussion prior to the event, please send it/them within the next two days.

→ *Au cas où vous envisageriez de soumettre un sujet ou une question avant la manifestation*

During this year-end review, I will share our business ***results to date***.

→ *résultats à la date d'aujourd'hui/à ce jour.*

Post-meeting notes should be sent by the end of this week so that we can complete the minutes/close the file/wrap up last minute details/ ***tie up loose ends***.

→ *régler les derniers détails.*

We do not have any topics "on the parking lot" for the team. ***All pending issues/outstanding issues have been resolved.***

→ *Tous les points en suspens sont réglés.*

Let's begin gathering information towards a KM strategy (Knowledge Management strategy).

→ *Il est temps de rassembler les informations en vue d'une stratégie de Gestion des Connaissances.*

IV. REVIEWING MODIFICATION ET VALIDATION DES DOCUMENTS

Please, amend and add to this agenda as you feel appropriate.

→ *Vous êtes invités à apporter les modifications que vous jugez utiles à l'ordre du jour.*

Please advise if you are not familiar with the team members and I will prepare their profiles for you.
➛ *Faites moi savoir si*

Let's discuss/do a brainstorming on ***refinements to the current blueprint***.
➛ *améliorations à apporter au projet actuel.*

Please find attached my attempt at the minutes of last Thursday's Bio meeting.Could you please ***correct the subjects which concern you and send me your modifications for consolidation***?
➛ *corriger les points de l'ordre du jour qui vous concernent et me renvoyer vos modifications en vue d'une version définitive ?*

Here is ***a second draft based on*** our discussion earlier today. Please feel free to make amendments. We may need to look at the impact of the latest budget.
➛ *une deuxième ébauche de proposition sur la base de*

Now that ***they are in receipt of*** the document, the personnel department will be able to review it at their convenience.
➛ *ils ont reçu*

I need to prepare a full job description ***which I will forward to you for your perusal***. Upon receipt of this document, can you please advise if it suits your requirements?
➛ *que je vous transmettrai pour que vous en preniez connaissance.*

Attached for your urgent attention is a draft regarding the next phase of the process.
➛ *Le projet que je joins a un caractère d'urgence et concerne la prochaine étape*

I think the document is ***great as is***.
➛ *parfait en l'état*

You are invited to ***write in your comments. Please use the space provided***.
➛ *ajouter vos commentaires dans l'espace réservé à cet effet.*

I have interlaced the paragraphs of your original e-mail with my comments, and have used a different colour to distinguish them.
➛ *j'ai intercalé mes propres commentaires dans le mail initial*

I'll suggest ***a few further parings down and minor revisions***.
➛ *réduire encore un peu le texte/l'élaguer et apporter quelques modifications mineures.*

I would appreciate another pair of eyes to look over the figures.
➛ *J'apprécierais le regard d'un tiers sur ces chiffres.*

I'd like to ***run everything past*** my manager before it reaches the CEO.
➛ *soumettre l'ensemble à*

V. PHOTOS PHOTOS

Hold it right there!
➛ *Ne bougez plus !*

No, I don't take a good photo.
➛ *Non, je ne suis pas photogénique.*

Can we all squeeze in a bit?
➛ *On peut se serrer un peu ?*

Can we have everybody for the photo?
➛ *Allez, tout le monde pour la photo !*

I'll go and ***round up the guests*** so that we can have a good photo shoot.
➛ *rassembler/regrouper les invités*

Events

Déjeuners et soirées

I. PREPARATION/PULLING TOGETHER AN EVENT
PRÉPARATION ET COORDINATION

I'd rather we didn't include a message with the invitation. I'll only be sending it to the team in the Paris area.

Please note that a message will be sent separately to those living in the Paris area and to those in other regions.

It's been decided to ***postpone the drinks party until January***.
➛ *reporter l'apéritif au mois de janvier.*

I just wanted to check with you ***if you see any barrier to moving forward with this dinner***, which I think will help recognise the team's accomplishments and build morale. Could you also confirm your availability?
➛ *si vous avez des objections à ce que nous donnions suite au dîner dont nous parlions*

I think it would be best to ***send out the invitation*** before Xmas to the respective teams.
➛ *lancer les invitations*

Do keep me posted about anything specific you'd like to include in the invitation. I'd just need to know before Thursday at the latest.
➛ *Pensez à me tenir au courant de*

Would you like a separate invitation for each team or ***would one invitation suffice***?
➛ *nous contenterons-nous d'une seule invitation ?*

It might be a better idea to have a buffet lunch rather than an evening event. ***As Tony and Hillary meet for regular updates on Tuesdays, this might be the ideal time to bring together both their teams.***
➛ *Nous pourrions profiter de la réunion hebdomadaire du mardi de Tony et Hillary pour rassembler leurs deux équipes.*

If we went for a buffet lunch, ***we might have a greater attendance/*** turnout.
➛ *peut-être aurions-nous un taux de participation plus élevé.*

If you require a reservation, we must ***act swiftly***, because January is in great demand.
➛ *agir sans tarder*

I think ***we can count on the basis of*** 60 to 70 people tbc (to be confirmed).
➛ *nous pouvons partir sur une base de*

Initially we could work on a basis of 60 to 70 people, ***subject to increase***.
➛ *mais ce chiffre peut augmenter.*

II. CHOOSING A VENUE
TROUVER LA BONNE ADRESSE ET LA COMMUNIQUER

I'd rather go off-site to make it a little bit more special/***I'd go for*** somewhere off-site.
➛ *Je serais partant(e) pour*

Having said that/that said, we need to find a suitable place (welcoming, good food, pleasant surroundings etc.).

I think it would be far more expensive ***if we were to go out*** as opposed to staying on site.
➛ *si nous devions déjeuner à l'extérieur*

There could be a problem with the venue: if all fails, could we hold it somewhere on the company restaurant premises?
➛ *Le lieu risque d'être problématique : au pire/dans le cas où aucune de nos pistes ne débouche, le déjeuner pourrait-il avoir lieu sur place/dans nos locaux ?*

Please check the possibility of a restaurant located between Lyon and Villefranche where we could get together in a more relaxed and friendly environment. ***I'm not sure if midday/noon or evening would be best.***

➛ *J'hésite encore entre un déjeuner et un dîner.*

Due to the outstanding results this last quarter, ***we should make a bit of a thing of it***. We need to check out some of the best restaurants.

➛ *on devrait fêter ça dignement.*

The estimate suits us, excluding the macarons, making a total of €412.

➛ *Le devis nous convient*

We are expecting around 35 people. What would your price be for champagne and ***finger food***?

➛ *amuse-gueules*

They don't break even.

➛ *Ils ne rentrent pas dans leurs frais.*

III. INVITATION TO BUSINESS BREAKFASTS, LUNCHES AND DINNERS

LES INVITATIONS

I have included/***You will find attached a map giving travel directions***

➛ *Dans la pièce jointe vous trouverez le plan d'accès.*

The RER, the metro or bus provide easy access to the restaurant.

➛ *Le restaurant est bien desservi par le RER et la RATP.*

A RER station, a metro station and a bus stop are ***all within easy reach of the restaurant***.

➛ *tous aisément accessibles à partir du restaurant.*

In recognition of everybody's hard work put in by everyone, Theo would like to invite you to a drinks party/to a « petit dej gourmand ».

➛ *À titre de remerciement pour le travail considérable fourni par chacun*

In appreciation for all your hard work and dedication over the past 6 months, ***we would like to extend an invitation to both teams***.
➛ *nous avons le plaisir d'inviter les deux équipes.*

To recognise/thank you for the effort you have contributed to the project, you are cordially invited to attend ***a drinks party*** on 17 February.
➛ *un apéritif*

Hopefully we will have the pleasure of your company.

Your presence would be greatly appreciated.

We do hope you will be able to join us/be able to attend.
➛ *Votre présence serait grandement appréciée.*

Ideally a 6.30 start would ***ensure that people would not arrive home too late*** for those with personal obligations.
➛ *permettrait aux invités de ne pas arriver trop tard chez eux*

A 6.30 start would be ideal, allowing those with personal obligations to leave early.
➛ *Commencer à 6 h 30*

It will begin at 6.30 pm and end at approximately 9.00 pm.

From 6.30 pm to 9 pm ***with perhaps a modest extension***.
➛ *et éventuellement un peu au-delà.*

The venue for the drinks party will be « Le Restaurant du Bout du Monde » on our Dunkirk site.
➛ *Le lieu retenu pour l'apéritif*

The drinks party will be held at « Le Restaurant du bout du Monde » on our Dunkirk site at 6 pm.
➛ *L'apéritif se tiendra*

This year, for a change, our annual drinks party ***will be held off-site***.
➛ *aura lieu hors site.*

We'll be meeting at "Le petit Gourmand" which ***is located at the following address***.
➛ *se trouve à l'adresse suivante.*

IV. LOGISTICS QUESTIONS PRATIQUES

Cloakroom facilities will be available.
➛ *Des vestiaires seront à disposition.*

You may find it difficult to park ***in the vicinity*** of the restaurant, and might like to take advantage of ***valet parking*** provided by the restaurant.
➛ *à proximité [...] service de voiturier*

For those interested in ***car pooling*** please let us know.
➛ *co-voiturage*

Should you require a taxi at the end of the evening, please let me know.
➛ *si vous souhaitez réserver un taxi*

V. AT THE RESTAURANT AU RESTAURANT

You'll find ***the seating plan*** just as you go into the dining room.
➛ *plan de table*

There's no seating plan, feel free to ***sit wherever you feel most comfortable***.
➛ *installez-vous où bon vous semble.*

You'll find your name on your ***place cards***.
➛ *marques-places*

I'm not sure ***the boy/girl seating arrangement is the best idea***.
➛ *que l'alternance homme/femme soit le placement le plus judicieux.*

Please, be sure to check ***the dress code*** for the evening event.
➛ *code vestimentaire/tenue protocolaire*

You can never ***be overdressed*** for this kind of event.
➛ *trop bien habillé*

Are you happy with ***the table you're on***?
➛ *la table à laquelle vous êtes placé(e) ?*

I'm being reasonable; ***I've been nursing the same drink all evening***.
➛ *j'ai toujours le même verre depuis le début de la soirée.*

Holidays

Congés, Noël et Nouvelle année

You haven't taken all your annual leave.

➛ *Tu n'as pas pris tous tes congés cette année.*

I'll mark Thursday 11 as a vacation day.

➛ *Je note le jeudi 11 comme étant un jour de congé.*

You have only used 75% of ***your vacation allowance***. You've got another 25% at your disposal/another 25% to take.

➛ *congés annuels*

They failed to take their full holiday entitlement and lost their remaining days.

➛ *Ils n'ont pas pris tous leurs congés et ils ont perdu des jours.*

Sam ***has stayed off work*** to help his wife/hasn't gone in/isn't coming in.

➛ *n'est pas venu au bureau*

I'll take Monday and Tuesday off in lieu of the weekend I worked.

➛ *Je vais prendre mes lundi et mardi pour récupérer le week-end où j'ai travaillé.*

Richard won't be available next Friday because ***he's making it a long weekend*** due to the Monday being a bank holiday.

➛ *il fait le pont*

I'm not sure how many ***compensation days*** I've got left.

➛ *RTT (Récupération du Temps de Travail)*

I'm owed a day, I've done lots of overtime.

➛ *On me doit un jour, j'ai fait beaucoup d'heures supplémentaires.*

I'm accumulating my compensation days for when my wife is on maternity leave.

➛ *Je garde mes RTT*

Because I've been ***on call*** so much as of late, the company owes me plenty of days/I have plenty of days' holiday to take/I'm owed many days.

➛ *d'astreinte*

We need to ***recap on people's holiday requests to make sure that someone's available to cover at all times.***

➛ *faire le point sur les congés des uns et des autres pour être sûrs qu'il y aura une permanence.*

Once the table has been completed by all team members, a rota will be drawn up to ensure the smooth running of the department/that there will be a minimum staff available to deal with emergencies.

➛ *Une fois le tableau rempli par tous, un roulement sera établi*

You need to ***complete***/fill in/fill out/***the attached chart with your holiday requirements***.

➛ *remplir le tableau avec vos demandes de congés.*

Please state your holiday requirements on the attached chart.

➛ *Veuillez indiquer vos demandes de congés*

A vacation planner will clearly set out who is in or out of the office during the summer break.

➛ *Grâce à un calendrier il sera aisé d'établir qui est en congé ou non pendant l'été.*

Our holidays are going to overlap. Let's hope that things tick over nicely.

➛ *Nos congés vont se chevaucher. Espérons que ça va bien se goupiller/que ça va bien marcher.*

Your holidays need to be staggered so that there is always someone here.

➛ *Il faut que vos congés soient échelonnés*

Children break up from school tomorrow.

➛ *L'école se termine demain/les enfants sont en vacances demain.*

My vacations often turn out to be ***a busman's holiday***, I'm afraid. I never completely switch my computer off.

➛ *vacances studieuses/boulot-boulot*

To welcome in the New Year and all the changes it will bring, Françoise would like to invite the team to a drinks party.

➛ *Pour accueillir la Nouvelle Année*

Let's ***ring out the old and ring in the new***, a drinks party has been organised for you!

➛ *fêtons le changement d'année*

After the ***over indulgences*** of Xmas, how about meeting over a coffee and pastries to exchange New Year wishes?

➛ *les quelques excès*

Ah well, one chapter closes, another opens.

We send our warmest wishes to you all for Christmas and the coming year.

I hope this letter finds you in good health, with your family around you for another wonderful holiday season.

Have a happy, safe holiday and a joyous New Year.

Where did the year go? Fast and furious and this year is showing no signs of being any different!

Last year introduced us to the "delights" of our number one project, and it looks like this year is going to be just as exciting. ***So let's brace ourselves for an eventful year!***

➛ *Préparons-nous à une année riche en évènements !*

I hope the New Year is treating you well.

The New Year will be upon us before we know it. It always comes around so fast.

➛ *La nouvelle année approche à grands pas. On ne voit pas le temps passer.*

With every good wish to you and your family for a blessed Christmas and a peaceful and fulfilling New Year.

Christmas has been and gone, and it's only now that I'm sending you words of seasonal cheer.

➛ *Noël est bien loin, et c'est avec quelque retard, que je vous présente mes voeux.*

Operating procedures

Procédures et règles internes

I. REQUESTS (FOR COMPUTER EQUIPMENT AND OTHERS)
DEMANDES DE MATÉRIEL

Could we envisage having another computer?

Some of my colleagues ***are in the dark as to when a repeat session is going to be held***. Are you counting on me to pass on the information or will you inform them directly?

➛ *s'interrogent sur la date d'une deuxième session/d'une session de rattrapage.*

Mr Schmidt ***requires your attention regarding the position of his computer screen in relation to the windows***.

➛ *vous soumet le problème qui le préoccupe actuellement concernant la position de son écran par rapport à la fenêtre.*

Can screen filters be adapted ***to cut out reflection***?

➛ *pour minimiser le phénomène de reflet.*

I am about to put in a purchase request for the company Miltus, formerly known as Laklis. Should we create a new entry in our database, or ***can we substitute one for the other***? As is often the case, this matter is somewhat urgent.

➛ *ou bien pouvons-nous remplacer l'un par l'autre ?*

I am of course at your disposal, should you require further information which may be pertinent to you.

Could you take a look at e-shopping to see ***where we're at with*** the request/to check how the request is coming along.

➛ *l'état d'avancement de*

On behalf of Sonia Parkinson, I wish to request access to Sharepoint.

➛ *Je m'adresse à vous de la part de Sonia Parkinson qui souhaite obtenir l'accès à*

In order ***to generate a new entry in our database***, we require the following: bank details, invoice or a bill, letter head. Could you please send them by return?
➛ *pour créer une nouvelle entrée dans notre de base de données*

II. POOLING INFORMATION
MUTUALISATION DES INFORMATIONS NUMÉRIQUES

Can you please ***set up a place on Sharepoint***, so that everyone on the team can have easy access to our weekly meeting reports?
➛ *créer un emplacement, un site sur Sharepoint*

This is the ideal tool for ***maintaining/updating/feeding our data base***.
➛ *entretenir notre base de données/la mettre à jour/l'alimenter*

You will now be able to ***open and read any of the documents*** relating to our last session and to post questions or comments you might have.
➛ *consulter tous les documents*

You can collect the data stored in Sharepoint. ***It can be used and added to easily.***
➛ *On peut l'utiliser et le compléter aisément.*

The resulting increase in "hits" ***raises your Google ranking***.
➛ *renforce votre positionnement dans Google.*

The hits our intranet site generates are vital to ratings and essential for the statistics we collect.
➛ *Le nombre de visites de notre intranet nous est indispensable pour estimer la fréquentation de notre site.*

We need to update ***our intranet feeds***.
➛ *actualiser nos données intranet.*

This is a site that will be added to on a regular basis.
➛ *Ce site pourra être alimenté au fur et à mesure.*

Traffic to the website has increased, which is very promising.

I am delighted to inform you all that our website is now up and running and can be accessed at www.dotdot.org. You will find a number of articles written by me (dotdotblog), as well as one under "…".

➛ *Nous avons le plaisir de vous annoncer que notre site internet est à présent pleinement opérationnel*

Please let me know what you think of the site if you take a look, ***or better still, submit a piece for future consideration and possible posting on the site***.

➛ *ou encore mieux, soumettez-nous un article pour que nous l'étudiions et que, le cas échéant, nous l'affichions sur le site.*

Click here to join the net meeting.

We taped the meeting and converted the files so that we can post them on the intranet on both sites.

➛ *nous avons enregistré la réunion*

How about using WinZip to send your files? It makes transportation and storage of your documents easier.

III. WORKFLOW PROCESSUS DE VALIDATION

To speed up your vacation request approval, I suggest we replace your current approver by Andrew. It can be done by the click of a button.

➛ *Afin d'accélérer la validation de votre demande de congé*

Your request ***will be okayed within twenty four hours***.

➛ *sera validée en 24 heures*

I am not yet signed in on all the systems and can't deal with stationery orders and purchase requests.

➛ *Je n'ai pas encore accès à toutes les applications et ne peux traiter ni les demandes de fournitures ni les demandes d'achats.*

If you attach a detailed sales proposal to your purchase request, it will be ***easier to get it past*** the financial controller.

➛ *plus facile de le faire valider par*

The number of procedural hoops one has to jump through to market a new product is mind-boggling!

➛ *La procédure pour commercialiser un nouveau produit est une véritable course d'obstacle, c'est effarant !*

IV. PASSES BADGES

In order to save Mr Alex Godwin time when he shows up at our Massy site, could we possibly ***activate his pass which is currently only set up for our Palaiseau site***?

➛ *activer son badge qui actuellement est configuré seulement pour notre site de Palaiseau ?*

Swipe your pass across the reader in order to access the building/ the premises.

➛ *Passez votre carte magnétique dans la fente du lecteur*

I'm not familiar with the ins and outs of access procedures.

➛ *Je ne suis pas très au fait du fonctionnement des procédures d'accès.*

As discussed please find below Melinda's details ***concerning the delivery of her security pass*** in readiness for her start date on 4 July.

➛ *pour la délivrance de son badge*

Access to the building may be arranged on her behalf, providing we have full details.

➛ *Ses droits d'accès peuvent être réglés sans qu'elle soit physiquement présente/peuvent être réglés à distance.*

Please ***hand in your pass to Security*** before you go.

➛ *remettez votre badge à la cellule sécurité*

This pass is time and date encoded.

It ceases to operate on departure or when cancelled.
➛ *Il cesse de fonctionner*

Hold the card to the panel/scan it across the reader ***for the door to slide open***.
➛ *Présentez la carte devant le lecteur magnétique et la porte coulissera.*

One important fact for car owners is that ***a sticker is mandatory*** for easy identification in case of a vehicle-related problem (lights left on, handbrake not on, etc.).
➛ *un macaron est obligatoire*

V. CONTRACTS (COORDINATION) SUIVI DE CONTRATS

The provider sends us his documents ***so that we can feed them into our database/to be fed into our database***.
➛ *pour que nous puissions alimenter notre base de données.*

A summary which shows the different stages of a contract or amendment ***as of when*** it arrives on the personal assistant's desk.
➛ *à partir du moment où*

The following is given only as a guideline and *is* ***in no way prescriptive***.
➛ *n'est en aucun cas normatif/obligatoire*

It shows the unavoidable steps ***to follow through the contracts/*** amendments before final agreement.
➛ *pour assurer le suivi des contrats*

It is important to ***meet a certain number of requirements***.
➛ *respecter un certain nombre d'exigences/de contraintes.*

You don't want your contract to ***be thrown out on a technicality***.
➛ *être rejeté pour vice de forme.*

A data chart must be completed for each specific purchase request, which must match the document requiring signature.
➛ *Pour chaque demande d'achat, une fiche de données doit être remplie et doit correspondre au document original destiné à la signature.*

The account's ***contact details*** should be shown.
➣ *les coordonnées*

We'll need the Purchase Department's ***go-ahead***.
➣ *feu vert*

Please check out ***the consistency in data*** (figures included) before I start processing the contract.
➣ *la cohérence des données*

I would like to remind you that ***unless an emergency dictates otherwise,*** it is essential that each step of the procedure should be scrupulously followed.
➣ *sauf en cas d'urgence*

Register the contract in the Contrat'Tech (here ***the contract number will be issued***).
➣ *un numéro de contrat sera attribué/y sera associé*

Submit the contract/amendment to Linda for signature.

Attach ***the approved documents*** to the purchase request (Contract/Sales Proposal/Purchase Department agreement).
➣ *documents validés*

Send the contract to the supplier and ***await its return***.
➣ *attendez qu'il vous soit retourné.*

Advise the Accounts Department to place the order with the supplier.
➣ *Avertissez la comptabilité que la commande peut être passée auprès du fournisseur.*

File the contract.
➣ *Archivez.*

Glitches

(Petits) problèmes techniques

The air conditioning ***is on the blink***. I'll pass this e-mail on to the technician for him to deal with it.

➛ *ne fonctionne pas/est HS (hors service)*

My computer***'s just gone down***, how long can I expect it to be before it is up and running again?

➛ *vient de tomber en panne*

I'm still ***in the throes of*** computer issues, and ***slowly going bananas***.

➛ *aux prises avec [...] je deviens chèvre.*

Your text message was incomplete. It read: "ABT2G CU@...", ***and then it broke off***.

➛ *et ensuite il est interrompu*

I seem to have lost the internet connection at the moment. Send your e-mail anyway and it will arrive when the connection is restored.

All machines give out eventually. After all, it was probably purchased about seven years ago.

➛ *Les machines ne sont pas éternelles.*

To think that we lose so much time a day to technological failures. ***I've had it with printers jamming and computers crashing!***

➛ *J'en ai assez des imprimantes qui bourrent et des ordinateurs qui plantent !*

Whatever way you look at it, whether it be on the fritz, on the blink, dodgy, out of order, etc. I can't get my computer started again. It just went kaput.

➛ *Dis-le comme tu veux, nase, pourri, HS, etc, mais je ne peux tout simplement pas faire redémarrer mon ordinateur.*

My message didn't send first time – technical fault obviously.

➣ *Mon message n'est pas parti du premier coup – défaillance technique/anomalie de toute évidence.*

Currently I cannot access the Ariba-Buyer application. ***I'm no longer in the system*** as they failed to renew my profile when they extended my contract.

➣ *Je n'ai plus de droits d'accès/je suis hors circuit*

During one hour this morning I experienced technical problems, therefore ***I have fallen behind with my workload***.

➣ *j'ai pris du retard dans mon travail*

The windstorm may have caused ***electrical outage***. That may be why ***her phone is ringing out***.

➣ *coupure de courant [...] son téléphone sonne dans le vide.*

She's had computer trouble and has been unable to send me the file ***so far***.

➣ *pour l'instant.*

A call has been placed with our IT Help Desk who are working for a resolve. Please accept our apologies.

➣ *Nous avons averti notre service d'assistance informatique qui s'efforce de résoudre le problème. Nous vous présentons nos excuses.*

... PART TWO ...

Talking the talk

Bien parler et menus propos

INTRODUCTION

Because my colleagues and I (basing what follows on my own experience) work within the same company, we perhaps mistakenly expect to think and communicate in the same way. But there are differences and competing interests within the various departments; recognising and respecting them can dramatically reduce confusion.

So for example, one of our rooms was locked one morning and happened to be needed urgently. In the absence of a spare, our only option was to ask our Security Unit on the floor below, to dispatch an agent to open it for us. My boss had ventured to call them a little earlier, but daunted by the impossibly long list of questions to answer, had gone back to attending to the very pressing matter of the "Comp Go-Live" which was threatening to collapse and was the reason why we so urgently needed the room. I was required to pursue where he had given up and dialled the 5 digits. The detached voice of an agent mechanically took me through a series of questions that might have been the stuff of an MI5 agent interrogation. Did I know the name of the usual occupant? What purpose was the room required for? Meanwhile I was trying to interpret what the frantic hand signals of my colleague in the doorway meant, suspecting it to be that panic was mounting. I dutifully answered the questions and sent an additional mail of confirmation as requested. We got the key.

At times a big company feels like an unwieldy piece of machinery and personal assistants far from playing a merely walk-on role, ensure that all its individual components work together well, even if they get tired of treading on eggshells sometimes and tip-toeing from one procedural minefield to another.

There is such a thing as company lingo, but it does not necessarily follow that people are bonded in a shared language. Our request had to be framed in a recognisable format and couched in words that were understood by the security agents. This sets out the case for facilitating communication in the workplace. By this I do not mean PR on a grand scale and the promotion of the company's culture and vision. I am referring to the way people talk to each other as a matter of routine or when clarity and accuracy of information is sought. Readers are invited to pick a journey through the phrases that crossed my own path and naturally found their way under the heading "Talking the talk". They are part of the armoury of any person living and working in a business community.

A number of them show close cooperation to be a valuable asset. Encouragement and appreciation are instrumental in building the positive frame of mind that will get people fired up and ready to resist the pressures of work. They contribute to positive and creative thinking within a company. In the course of my various assignments, I have come upon words that achieved this effect. They are featured in this selection and are the perfect vehicle to promote collaborative work and enhance people's awareness of the value of their contribution to the company.

Clarifying

Clarifier

For trip planning purposes, you need to know that the previous message wasn't clear. ***We meant to say*** Malcom should go directly to the office and not the hotel.

➛ *Ce qu'il fallait entendre c'est que/Notre intention était de dire que*

For clarification's sake, can you please send us your flight number and arrival time?

➛ *Pour éviter tout malentendu/par souci de clarté*

I am glad ***we have everything all squared away***.

➛ *que nous ayons tout bouclé.*

After a lot of discussion about this complicated issue, we finally ***have it all straightened out***!

➛ *tout est réglé/les choses sont claires !*

Will you be able to ***walk me through*** the presentation? It's above my head and way too dense for me to understand it.

➛ *me briefer/m'expliquer le contenu/me montrer en quoi consiste*

"Save-the-date" invites will go out to the President and Vice President.

➛ *Des pré-invitations seront lancées auprès du Président*

Space permitting, invites may go out to some area managers.

➛ *En fonction des places disponibles certains responsables peuvent recevoir des invitations.*

We currently have ***a rolling list*** of 50 targets which is updated on a monthly basis.

➛ *liste évolutive, à mettre régulièrement à jour*

I've gone with your rough estimate of attendees; should there be any spare places I have drawn up a separate list of Paris-based employees who could fill the gaps.

➛ *Je me suis basée sur le nombre approximatif de participants que vous prévoyez ; au cas où il resterait des places, j'ai dressé une liste des salariés dépendant de Paris qui pourraient les remplir.*

While we aim to be as transparent as possible there are some elements of our discussions that need to be kept confidential. Members must handle sensitive information carefully.

➛ *Nous visons la transparence, cependant,*

In my layperson's view, this was not a simple switch to make.

➛ *Pour le béotien/le profane que je suis*

I made it very clear that you (and other stakeholders) need to be involved in these discussions and was assured that you would be.

➛ *J'ai été très explicite sur le fait que*

I'm about to order business cards for Mr Parker, and have noticed an anomaly with the company logo. Could you please confirm that the latest design is available online?

I haven't heard back, ***so I assume that*** all is in order.

➛ *j'en conclus donc que*

You will find the answers to the most frequently asked questions on our website under ***Q&A***.

➛ *Questions/Réponses*

The baseline is that failing the CEO's presence the kick-off meeting cannot go ahead.

➛ *Le fond du problème c'est qu'en l'absence du PDG*

The sales proposal currently shows working hours and daily rates. This must be avoided; the reason being that commercial ***stakes*** differ from legal stakes.

➛ *les enjeux*

I think ***they've misconstrued*** the idea behind the restructuring plan.
➣ *ils ont mal interprété*

A lot of change management skills will be required ***for the message to sink in***.
➣ *pour que le message soit pleinement compris.*

This will be "work in progress" but I want to ***touch base with you on this topic*** as we get closer to the launch.
➣ *prendre contact avec vous à ce sujet*

I had to carry out several checks, ***hence the delay***.
➣ *d'où le retard/de ce fait, j'ai pris du retard.*

Let me set the record straight about the mislaid document; it's never passed this way!
➣ *Que les choses soient claires, je n'ai jamais eu le document égaré entre les mains !*

I'd like to ***let you know where we stand*** on the Minusmess contract.
➣ *vous tenir au courant de notre position*

A few things ***need to be seen/need your attention before approval***.
➣ *doivent être portées à votre attention avant approbation du dossier.*

The reason why I'm sending the contract back, is that ***the quote shows working hours and daily rates***; this must be avoided.
➣ *l'estimation indique les heures travaillées et les taux journaliers*

Hopefully the above ***procedure will help us to be finely tuned*** and therefore lead us to save time and gain in efficiency.
➣ *la procédure telle qu'elle est exposée nous permettra d'accorder nos violons/d'être bien en phase*

Connecting people

Mettre en relation

I. ACTING AS AN INTERMEDIARY SERVIR D'INTERMÉDIAIRE

Perhaps I can help you ***reach out to*** the right person within Gremkol to deal with this request.
➣ *joindre/vous rapprocher de*

It came about that I received a request which I believe was meant for you.
➣ *Il se trouve que j'ai reçu une demande, qui me semble-t-il, vous était adressée.*

Could we possibly ***redirect the purchase request to*** somebody who would sort it out?
➣ *réorienter la demande d'achat vers*

I have a request ***on behalf of*** Ms Nagel and I'm not sure to whom I should address this.
➣ *de la part de*

I will be happy to ***put you on to*** the person who is most likely to be of assistance here.
➣ *vous mettre en relation avec*

You are probably ***in a better position*** than I am to deal with this.
➣ *mieux placé(e)*

They are looking to speak with someone who has established links with universities abroad. I thought ***you were best suited to*** talk to them.
➣ *Ils souhaitent s'adresser à […] que vous étiez la personne la mieux à même de*

I will pass the information along to our team members.

I will head our sales efforts along with Kevin and will ***act as a conduit for*** you to our team here in the US regarding the current domestic evaluation.

➛ *servir d'intermédiaire*

Is there ***someone else in your organisation that you would recommend we reach out to***?

➛ *une personne dans votre société qui serait susceptible de prendre en compte notre requête ?*

Catherine and I will coordinate with regards to your transportation and hotel.

I've heard back from Sam and thought ***you would like me to fill you in on what he said***.

➛ *tu voudrais que je te tienne au courant de ce qu'il a dit.*

II. INTERNET LINKS SUIVEZ LE LIEN !

They have ***a careers section specifically targeting international internships*** – the links below will take you there.

➛ *un service orientation spécialement consacré aux stages à l'international*

Please see the Net Meeting Link below for our teleconference, which will take place on Tuesday 8 December in Frankfurt. The link will be open from 8.30 am to 5.30 pm.

Check out the message I sent to Patrick by clicking on the link.

➛ *Consultez*

III. CC METTRE EN COPIE

I have cc'd Kevin in this e-mail in an effort to coordinate a convenient time to meet.

➛ *J'ai mis Kevin en copie, pour tenter de faire coïncider nos emplois du temps et prendre rendez-vous.*

I have copied her into this e-mail.

Let me know if you want to be cc'd on all of them or if you'd rather we didn't ***clog your inbox***.

➛ *encombrer ta messagerie.*

Please forward this message to anyone I might have inadvertently left off this mailing list and to anyone else on your teams who should get this news.

➛ *Veuillez transmettre ce mail à toute personne que j'aurais omise de la liste par mégarde*

I apologise if some people have not been copied in. Not being fully acquainted with all of the team yet, I would ask you to kindly forward the present invitation ***to anyone I have missed out***.

➛ *toute personne que j'aurais oubliée/que j'aurais manqué d'inclure.*

I have used a pre-set address list, ***so that nobody gets cut out of the loop*** by mistake. But feel free to add anyone you think should be included.

➛ *afin que personne ne soit exclu de la boucle*

Members of the team who are copied into this e-mail ***will be aware that this is a matter of utmost urgency***.

➛ *sauront que cette question doit être traitée en priorité/ceci est une question d'urgence absolue.*

Being positive

Être positif et savoir le dire

I. THANKS REMERCIER

The beautiful scarf you so generously gave me continues to be a reminder of our time together ***and I cherish it***. Thank you.

➛ *et elle m'est précieuse.*

"Pleased" doesn't get close. I'm positively over the moon with your present.

➛ *Dire que je suis « ravie » serait une litote, je suis tout simplement comblée.*

I would like to thank you from the bottom of my heart for your lovely gifts which I greatly appreciate.

I appreciate your kind gesture. You couldn't have chosen better.

Just to say thank you for the lovely meal we shared with the rest of the team. Great choice!

II. APPRECIATION OF HARD WORK RECONNAÎTRE LE TRAVAIL ACCOMPLI

I appreciate your time and follow-through here. Just let me know what works for the others.

➛ *Merci pour le temps que vous avez consacré au suivi de ce dossier. Dites-moi tout simplement ce qui convient le mieux aux uns et aux autres.*

I appreciate your continued patience; your help has been invaluable!

We owe it to your in-depth knowledge of the Paris area, that our visitor made it to the airport in time.

➛ *Votre longue expérience de la région parisienne nous a été d'un grand secours. Sans vous notre invité ne serait jamais arrivé à temps à l'aéroport.*

The cocktail party was a huge success. ***Please thank the whole of the catering team on our behalf.***

➛ *Veuillez remercier l'ensemble de l'équipe de restauration de notre part.*

We have had quite good feedback from our guests and would like to thank all the people involved in this success.

➛ *Nous avons eu d'excellents retours/des commentaires flatteurs de la part de nos hôtes*

This seminar ***has been no mean achievement***. This is largely due to your close cooperation and flexibility.

➛ *n'a pas été un moindre exploit/était loin d'être gagné d'avance*

Your catering team has been more than professional in accommodating our demands and needs, not to mention having to bear with a delayed payment. We are very grateful.

➛ *Votre personnel de restauration s'est montré d'un grand professionnalisme, attentif et disponible, sans parler de la patience que notre règlement différé lui a demandé.*

Thank you so much for your prompt action.

➛ *Nous vous remercions de votre réactivité.*

We are indebted to you for fast-tracking this visa request. Lionel would not have made it to Shanghai this time around.

➛ *Nous vous savons gré d'avoir accéléré le processus de validation de cette demande de visa.*

Many thanks for your efficiency in putting my file on the top of your pile and for giving it immediate attention upon arrival.

We thank you for pursuing the matter and are grateful for the end result – I did get a refund eventually!

➛ *Merci d'avoir assuré le suivi de cette affaire, l'issue en a été heureuse – j'ai enfin obtenu le remboursement !*

Completing this project in good time certainly ***won him a few Brownie points***.

➛ *lui a fait marquer des points*

Your idea of placing freebies in each hotel room ***went down a treat***.
➛ *a eu un franc succès.*

III. PRAISING PEOPLE FÉLICITER

They were ably assisted by our outstanding staff.
➛ *Ils ont bénéficié en cela de l'assistance experte de notre personnel.*

You're a legend!

You're a gem.

Sometimes there aren't enough gold stars in the world!

A +, Deborah!
➛ *20/20, Deborah !*

This is an excellent piece of research, as we normally expect from Mandy.
➛ *L'étude est excellente, nous n'en attendions pas moins de la part de Mandy.*

IV. LOOKING ON THE BRIGHT SIDE VOIR LE BON CÔTÉ DES CHOSES

The agenda for the day's event ***is really starting to come together***.
➛ *commence vraiment à prendre forme/à se profiler/à se dessiner.*

My organisation chart is taking shape nicely; I should be able to present it to the team shortly.
➛ *Mon organigramme a bien avancé*

By some miracle of scheduling, it seems that both Linda and Charles will be in the US at the same time.
➛ *Par un hasard providentiel les calendriers de Linda et Charles font qu'ils se trouveront aux US tous les deux au même moment.*

We now have the names of a handful of people at the Help desk, ***which is a step up from when we arrived!***
➛ *ce qui représente un progrès par rapport à notre arrivée !*

We're making headway towards hiring a temporary replacement. HR should be giving us the go-ahead soon.

➛ *Nous sommes en passe d'embaucher un intérimaire/Notre démarche pour l'embauche d'un intérimaire est bien engagée.*

We've made excellent progress so far. All the software applications ***will be up and running*** for the official launch at the beginning of next month.

➛ *seront opérationnelles*

We really had ***a slap-up meal***. Heaven will be a letdown after that!

➛ *repas excellent.*

I trust that your office move was trouble-free/***went without any hitches***.

➛ *s'est déroulé sans anicroches.*

I appreciate how diaries are a moving event and I am quite happy to modify the agenda accordingly.

➛ *Je sais bien que les calendriers ne sont jamais complètement figés ; je suis donc prêt à modifier l'ordre du jour en conséquence.*

It's up to the individual to make what he/she wants of the position; ***it's far from a dead-end job***!

➛ *un métier qui offre de belles perspectives d'avenir !*

Over time, ***I'll grow into the job***. I know there's a lot to learn before I am fully functional.

➛ *je vais prendre mes marques/apprendre les ficelles peu à peu.*

V. REMAINING POSITIVE IN SPITE OF SMALL HICCUPS
RESTER ZEN MALGRÉ LES IMPRÉVUS

The move went smoothly. However, I notice that my printer hasn't arrived yet.

➛ *Le déménagement s'est fort bien déroulé.*

Our team has just moved in, and all went well. ***There are a few teething troubles*** however which require your attention.

➛ *Il y a quelques difficultés de mise en route*

It's been a hard slog but the positive news is: everyone is up and running on the new site!

➛ *On a vraiment peiné/galéré*

I'd like to frame it all with more positive news, but due to delays in the completion of the project, on-duty calls are still on the cards.

➛ *J'aimerais vous présenter la chose sous un jour plus favorable, mais le projet ayant pris quelque retard, les astreintes sont toujours d'actualité/ne sont pas exclues.*

The chocolates left on desks as a welcome gesture were much appreciated. Could we possibly have ***two more of the same for Mrs Lacey and Mr Phillips who appear to have been left out***?

➛ *deux supplémentaires pour Mme Lacey et M. Phillips qui paraissent avoir été oubliés ?*

"Facilitators"

Les mots qui favorisent les échanges

I. WORDS OF GREETING LES MOTS POUR ACCUEILLIR

I hope this message finds you well, refreshed from vacation ***and not overwhelmed***.

➣ *et pas submergé(e) de travail/et pas trop surchargé(e).*

How have you been?

➣ *Alors, quelles sont les nouvelles ?*

I hope ***you're on top of this morning's events*** at Tazina and co.

➣ *que tu envisages la matinée avec sérénité/que tu ne te laisses pas dépasser par les évènements*

I hope all is going well with you.

I hope all is well, and that ***you're not sinking under loads of work.***

➣ *que vous ne croulez pas sous le poids du travail.*

I'm fine, thanks, the better for seeing you/hearing your voice.

➣ *Je vais bien, merci, d'autant mieux que j'ai le plaisir de vous voir/de vous entendre au bout du fil.*

I hope your first day back hasn't been too much of a shock to the system.

➣ *J'espère que votre reprise n'a pas été trop traumatisante.*

Welcome and please let me know if you should need anything at all!

II. WORDS OF ENCOURAGEMENT LES MOTS QUI ENCOURAGENT

Come on***, where's your fight!***

➣ *je t'ai connu plus pugnace !*

You keep that chin up, hey?
➛ *Allez, haut les cœurs !/Ne te laisse pas abattre !*

Come on***, the fight's not over yet!***
➛ *tu n'as pas dit ton dernier mot !*

Don't let it get to you.
➛ *Ne t'en fais pas pour ça/il ne faut pas que cela t'affecte/te touche.*

Everything will turn out ok, just wait and see.
➛ *Tout va bien se passer/s'arranger, tu verras.*

There's bound to be a brilliant turn of events soon.
➛ *C'est sûr qu'il va y avoir une issue positive.*

III. PARTING WORDS LES MOTS POUR PRENDRE CONGÉ

Again, ***we look forward to furthering our discussion with you and your team***.
➛ *nous serons ravis de poursuivre la discussion avec votre équipe et vous-même.*

Have a lovely weekend if I don't "talk" to you before that!

No doubt we will cross paths and it will be a pleasure to see you again.
➛ *Nos chemins se croiseront sans doute de nouveau*

I'm keeping my fingers crossed on your behalf.

Drop us a mail!

Keep in touch!

Don't be a stranger.
➛ *N'oublie pas de nous faire signe/de te manifester.*

Catch you soon!

See you around!

All good wishes and thanking you in anticipation for your reply.

Best to say that we'll hook up at the end of the month.
➛ *Il est plus sage de prendre rendez-vous pour la fin du mois.*

Hope our paths will cross in the corridors of Tazina and Co before long.

We'll make a date before we go.

Mind how you go with your suitcase!
➛ *Faites attention à ne pas trébucher avec votre valise !*

IV. THE READY WORD LES MOTS PASSE-PARTOUT

Never a dull moment!
➛ *On ne s'ennuie pas ici !*

No problems, ***all part of the service!***
➛ *je suis là pour ça !*

Spot on!
➛ *Tout à fait/très juste/bien vu !*

You should be so lucky!
➛ *Ce serait trop beau !*

I'll hold you to that!
➛ *Je vous prends au mot !*

More's the pity!
➛ *Grand dommage ! 3 fois hélas !*

I'll be sure to do that!
➛ *Je n'y manquerai pas !*

Too right we will!
➛ *Et comment on le fera !/y a intérêt !*

It seems that way.
➛ *J'en ai bien l'impression.*

I'll put my mind to it.
➣ *Je vais y réfléchir.*

I'll get thinking.
➣ *Il faudra que j'y réfléchisse.*

That figures.
➣ *Je comprends maintenant.*

It stands to reason.
➣ *Cela va de soi.*

O God, ***is there no hiding place!***
➣ *je ne sais plus où me mettre !*

Why he came to mind was because…
➣ *Ce pour quoi j'ai pensé à lui/ce qui m'a fait penser à lui…*

You speak truer than you know.
➣ *Vous ne croyez pas si bien dire.*

Never was a truer word spoken.
➣ *Jamais on n'a dit plus vrai.*

It's all in a day's work.
➣ *Ça finira par se faire/ça fait partie du travail.*

Answers on a postcard, please!
➣ *Si quelqu'un a la réponse, prière de nous le faire savoir !*

I'll toss you for it.
➣ *On se fait ça à pile ou face ?*

You kept this quiet!
➣ *Tu nous avais caché ça !*

First I've heard!
➣ *C'est la première fois que j'en entends parler !*

V. WORDS THAT CONNECT LES MOTS POUR GARDER CONTACT

I am sorry I cannot bring you better news but I hope you understand.

Thanks for getting back to me.
➛ *Je vous remercie de revenir vers moi.*

Have you had any thoughts about...?
➛ *Tu as pu réfléchir un peu à... ?*

Excuse me looking at my watch. ***I don't mean to be rude; it's just that I have/I'm expected in another meeting following on from this one.***
➛ *je ne veux pas être désagréable, c'est juste que je suis attendu dans un autre meeting.*

Sorry for sounding a bit rushed when we just spoke, but a rush job had just come up.
➛ *Désolé(e) d'avoir eu l'air un peu pressé là tout de suite, mais il nous a fallu régler une urgence.*

I have quite ***a healthy crop of e-mails*** myself!
➛ *une belle collection de mails*

If you're looking for quality service, then look no further.
➛ *Si vous cherchez un service de qualité, alors ne cherchez plus/vous êtes au bon endroit.*

Sorry, 34 not 35: ***one number out.***
➛ *je me suis trompé(e) d'un chiffre.*

Enjoying a blessed moment of relaxation.
➛ *Je savoure les bienfaits d'un moment de détente.*

Your reputation precedes you.

Monday morning feeling.

May Friday hurry up and get here!
➛ *Vivement vendredi !*

TGIF (=Thank God it's Friday).

Roll on Friday/the end of the week!
➛ *Vivement vendredi !*

Just in case, on an outside chance, I might think of a solution to Anna's last minute hotel room reservation problem.
➛ *Au cas où, on ne sait jamais, il m'arriverait de trouver une solution à*

VI. TIMING JE NE VOUS DÉRANGE PAS ?

I'm sorry to trouble you so early.
➛ *Désolé(e) de vous importuner si tôt.*

Hope we're not catching you at the wrong time.
➛ *Peut-être n'est-ce pas le bon moment pour vous appeler/pour passer ?*

I hope it isn't an inconvenient time.
➛ *Peut-être n'est-ce pas l'heure idéale pour vous appeler/pour passer ?*

VII. WORDS OF WISDOM PAROLES DE SAGESSE

Good things come to those who wait.
➛ *Patience et longueur de temps…*

Patience is a virtue.

Let well alone = the perfect is the enemy of the good
➛ *Le mieux est l'ennemi du bien.*

If you can't do great things, do little things in a great way

You only fail if you stop trying

Many a mickle makes a muckle.
➛ *Les petits ruisseaux font les grandes rivières.*

Let's not run ahead/Let's not get ahead of ourselves.
➛ *Ne nous emballons pas/pas de précipitation.*

VIII. THE WEATHER QUAND ON PARLE MÉTÉO

The sky looks ***unpromising***.
➣ *Le ciel est peu prometteur/n'annonce rien de bon.*

There are ***fair weather clouds***.
➣ *nuages de beau temps*

We are having ***ropey weather***.
➣ *temps moche*

It's spotting.
➣ *Il commence à y avoir des gouttes.*

It's lashing down.
➣ *Il pleut des cordes.*

The rain is coming down in stair rods.
➣ *Il y a une pluie battante.*

The rain is showing signs of easing off.
➣ *Il a l'air de pleuvoir un peu moins/la pluie a l'air de se calmer un peu.*

The sun ***is struggling here.***
➣ *a du mal à percer.*

If the fog comes down, we are in for long delays on the roads.
➣ *Si le brouillard tombe, on n'échappera pas à des ralentissements sur les routes.*

The fog was so thick, I couldn't see further than my nose.

The fog has finally lifted, but it was quite dense this morning.
➣ *Le brouillard a fini par se lever*

A heck of a wind is getting up.
➣ *Le vent se lève et il va être mordant/vif.*

Going outside chills you to the bone.
➣ *Dès que tu sors tu es gelé.*

The snow is lying.

→ *La neige tient.*

Well, summer is in retreat, although it never really arrived.

→ *L'été touche à sa fin, bien qu'il n'ait jamais vraiment commencé/ bien qu'il ne soit jamais vraiment arrivé.*

If it fairs up and the sun comes out, Paris's outbound traffic is going to be terrible this week end.

→ *Si le temps s'adoucit et que le soleil se montre*

IX. HEALTH QUAND ON PARLE SANTÉ

a) Doctors, prescriptions and sick leaves Médecins, ordonnances et congés maladie

Whatever the doctor heard at my appointment yesterday made him nervous enough to ask me to ***get some x-rays*** and some blood tests today...

→ *faire faire des radios*

Apparently there is some fluid on my chest and the CAT scan (Computerised Axial Tomography) indicated ***a lot of build-up in my sinus*** and nasal passages.

→ *un engorgement des sinus*

They think ***"my cold" has shifted to light walking pneumonia***.

→ *mon prétendu rhume a évolué en pneumonie atypique.*

Outside of being exhausted, the nice thing is that ***after the IV*** (intravenous) ***they put me on***, I feel a lot better!!

→ *après qu'ils m'ont mis(e) sous perfusion*

After a discussion with the doctor, ***I'm coming into work*** but going to take it extremely easy this week, cancelling all my after work and weekend engagements and just rest for most of next week.

→ *je viens au bureau*

He's called in sick.

➛ *Il a appelé pour dire qu'il était malade/qu'il ne venait pas au bureau.*

I've taken my first dose of antibiotics and ***once they kick in*** I should be okay by tomorrow.

➛ *une fois qu'ils commenceront à faire effet*

Ian is working from home and ***very medicated***.

➛ *a une forte dose de médicaments/un traitement lourd*

The doctor thinks I have an acute sinus infection with ***the beginnings of a strep throat***.

➛ *les signes précurseurs d'une angine*

She's been through the mill.

➛ *Elle en a vu de dures/elle a passé une période très éprouvante.*

Things are looking up, though it is taking longer than I thought to recover from the operation.

➛ *Les choses vont mieux*

The plaster comes off tomorrow. This should make life considerably easier.

➛ *On m'enlève le plâtre demain.*

She has developed a neck condition from sitting too long hours at her computer.

➛ *Elle a attrapé un torticolis à force de*

He's rallied a little. He's still fairly weak, though.

➛ *Il a un peu repris du poil de la bête.*

It is the first time I've been absent through illness.

➛ *Je n'avais jamais pris de congé de maladie.*

As things stand, I'm in the clear; I'll have to make ***a follow-up appointment***, though.

➛ *rendez-vous de suivi*

He is very much improved.
➛ *Son état de santé est bien meilleur.*

You'll soon be completely restored.
➛ *Vous serez bientôt tout à fait rétabli.*

Her heart could not keep up with her ***compromised lungs*** after years of smoking.
➛ *poumons en mauvais état*

b) Small talk about more ordinary ailments
Papotages autour d'ennuis de santé bénins

I feel ***a bit ropey***. I could do with a strong coffee.
➛ *un peu patraque.*

I feel ***fit to drop***.
➛ *claqué(e)/épuisé(e).*

I had a wakeful night, probably as a result of this visa business that's been giving me grief lately.
➛ *J'ai mal dormi, sans doute à cause de ce problème de visa qui m'a contrarié.*

Feel ***out of sorts***/under the weather/washed out/out of shape.
➛ *pas dans mon assiette.*

He is in rude health.
➛ *Il a une santé de fer.*

She's blooming/she looks a picture of health.
➛ *Elle est resplendissante.*

It was essential ***to get the batteries going again***.
➛ *de recharger les batteries.*

Once you've put it on (weight) it's difficult to get rid of it/ to shift it.
➛ *Une fois qu'on a pris les kilos il est difficile de s'en débarrasser.*

Your fit of giddiness is a symptom of fatigue after the week's work.

➣ *Vos vertiges sont symptomatiques d'un état de fatigue lié à tout le travail de la semaine.*

c) Colds
Coups de froid

I'm pretty bunged up, I can't shift this cold.

➣ *J'ai le nez complètement bouché, je ne peux pas me débarrasser de ce rhume.*

I've got the sniffles.

➣ *Je sens un rhume qui vient/je renifle.*

I can't stop sniffing.

➣ *Je n'arrête pas de renifler.*

I can't shake off this cold.

➣ *Je ne peux pas me débarrasser de ce rhume.*

I must have been at the tail end of the cold.

➣ *J'ai dû arriver à la fin de l'épidémie de rhume.*

I've got the shivers, it could be the start of a cold.

➣ *J'ai des frissons*

The cold ***has gone onto my chest***.

➣ *est descendu sur la poitrine.*

I'm aching all over, maybe I'm coming down with flu'.

➣ *J'ai mal partout, si ça se trouve, je couve une grippe.*

I'm feeling a little ***drubbed***.

➣ *un peu courbaturé(e).*

Hope ***your cold hasn't developed any further***.

➣ *Ton rhume n'a pas évolué.*

I felt a bit rough yesterday, but my cold is clearly on the mend. Everybody's got it at the moment.
➛ *J'étais mal fichu(e) hier*

d) Other
Autre

When her results are through, she will have to make an appointment with a specialist.
➛ *Une fois qu'elle aura reçu les résultats*

Now the problems with her arthritic left knee ***are starting to take their toll***, preventing her from getting around.
➛ *commencent à se faire sentir, à lui coûter*

This summer he had ***a right knee replacement***.
➛ *une prothèse du genou droit.*

She is planning to have the other knee replaced this next June. Then she'll be as good as new.

My eye problem ***put me out of action*** for a while. But things are back to normal.
➛ *m'a mis(e) hors circuit*

My knee is giving me gyp.
➛ *Mon genou me fait horriblement mal/me fait vivre un enfer.*

She needs to be looked over after her fall. I'll call the infirmary.
➛ *Il faut qu'elle aille montrer ça/qu'un médecin l'examine.*

Her ankle has ballooned.
➛ *Sa cheville a doublé de volume.*

The swelling has gone down.
➛ *Ça a désenflé un peu.*

I made an appointment for a blood test early tomorrow morning as it has to be ***"nil by mouth"***.
➛ *à jeun.*

HR and communication

RH et communication

I. THE CANDIDATE LE CANDIDAT ET SON CV

a) Introduces him/herself
Se présenter

I have a degree from a British University.

➣ *J'ai obtenu ma licence dans une université britannique.*

I am due to undertake further studies in the form of a diploma to broaden my understanding in this area, develop new skills and build relationships.

➣ *J'ai prévu de poursuivre des études diplômantes, mon but étant d'approfondir mes connaissances dans ce domaine*

Since completing a PhD in pharmacology, I have spent over 15 years in life sciences and healthcare communications.

➣ *Une fois mon doctorat terminé*

I am well-grounded in neuro-science.

➣ *J'ai une formation solide*

I am responsible for engaging employees in the strategic plans of the organisation through workshops and brainstorming sessions.

➣ *Mon rôle est d'encourager les salariés à être partie prenante des/à prendre une part active aux décisions stratégiques de notre entreprise*

A further element of my role is promoting/seeking partnerships with Universities abroad.

➣ *Autre aspect de mon rôle, je promeus*

I joined the company as Human Resources manager two years ago before taking on a wider role as European HR Manager earlier this year.

➣ *J'ai rejoint la société en tant que directeur des ressources humaines il y a deux ans et au début de cette année mes fonctions se sont étendues à celles de directeur des ressources humaines chargé de l'Europe.*

I have worked in a variety of senior Communications and Public Affairs roles.

My other duties involve dealing with charity support.

➣ *Je suis également responsable du soutien à des œuvres caritatives.*

I also contribute to intranet publishing.

➣ *Je collabore également aux publications intranet.*

I want a job ***with more scope***.

➣ *plus ambitieux.*

This is a job for which I think I am ideally suited.

➣ *Je pense correspondre parfaitement à ce poste.*

I think ***your job offers just the right match for my skills and interests***.

➣ *le poste correspond en tous points à mes compétences et à ma spécialité.*

I wish to further my experience in the field of animal health care.

➣ *Je souhaite aller plus avant*

I believe there is scope in your company for me to follow my professional ambitions/line of expertise/interest/what I have started.

➣ *À n'en pas douter votre société offre des perspectives d'avenir pour/me permettra de réaliser mes objectifs professionnels.*

I now wish to relocate to Western Europe on a permanent basis.

This position would make it possible for me to bring my own skills and corporate experience to your company.

➛ *Ce poste permettrait de mettre mon expérience et mes compétences au service de votre société.*

I'm a career changer from computer programming.

➛ *J'ai quitté la programmation informatique et me suis reconverti(e).*

b) Is recommended by his/her manager
Être recommandé(e) par son/sa responsable

Highly analytical and insightful, Estelle brings a fresh and valid perspective to each project.

➛ *Estelle possède un sens fort de l'analyse et sait approfondir. Elle porte un regard neuf sur chacun des projets et sa contribution est de qualité.*

Eleanor shares her opinions with authority and dedication ***to the most positive outcome possible***.

➛ *pour un résultat optimal.*

She has quickly brought her academic credentials to fruit in a consulting environment.

➛ *Elle a su rapidement tirer parti de ses diplômes universitaires*

She ***has won her colleagues' trust*** and has become indispensable to the team.

➛ *a su gagner la confiance de ses collègues*

She made a niche for herself and has become a valued member of our team.

➛ *Elle a su s'intégrer/trouver sa place*

Michael rapidly ***worked his way up through the ranks*** and is now regarded as a leading expert in our line of business.

➛ *a gravi les échelons*

Having rotated within the company, Ruth has a thorough knowledge of how we work.

➛ *Ayant occupé des postes divers au sein de notre entreprise, Ruth connaît parfaitement notre mode de fonctionnement.*

He is ***a live member of my department***, and I would highly recommend him.

➛ *membre dynamique/très présent de mon service*

II. RECRUITMENT RECRUTEMENT

This will ***reinforce the company's profile as a key player in the field of public health***.

➛ *promouvoir l'image de notre société dans son rôle clé/comme acteur privilégié de la santé publique.*

There's ***a vacuum of competence*** here, we need to start recruiting.

➛ *une carence en compétence*

As the context has changed, so have the recruiting criteria.

Casting the net wide increases the chances of landing an impressive catch.

➛ *Ratisser large/élargir notre champ de recrutement*

LIFO: Last In First Out.

The pay is the job's big draw.

➛ *Ce qui fait l'attraction du poste, c'est le salaire.*

There are ***no openings right now***.

➛ *aucun poste à pourvoir actuellement.*

Recruitment has been put on hold for now. Neither permanent nor fixed term contracts are available.

➛ *Le recrutement est en suspens/gelé, qu'il s'agisse de CDI ou de CDD.*

You can't just wheel out a replacement. There's a procedure to follow.

➣ *Tu ne peux pas te contenter de faire venir un remplaçant. C'est toute une procédure.*

We had one no-show.

➣ *Une personne ne s'est pas présentée à l'entretien.*

Could you e-mail your CV over to us?

People have to understand that ***you can't get into a desired job function right away.***

➣ *on ne peut pas tout de suite accéder au poste auquel on aspire.*

III. JOB DESCRIPTION PROFIL DE POSTE

You will be expected to work seamlessly with our colleagues abroad and interface with global communications and media relations teams.

➣ *On attendra de vous de travailler de manière fluide avec*

We would be looking for you to provide original, creative work on the design of the plan.

➣ *Nous attendons de vous une approche originale et novatrice*

If there are specific areas that you wish to be involved in, please let me know.

➣ *S'il y a des domaines particuliers auxquels vous souhaitez participer/ des aspects de la vie de notre organisation auxquels vous souhaitez vous joindre*

Soft skills such as communication and team work will be essential to the job.

➣ *compétences relationnelles*

IV. TERMS OF CONTRACT LES TERMES D'UN CONTRAT

The hours will be flexible as most networking events will be outside of office hours.

You will be ***reimbursed for all out-of-pocket expenses*** such as local travel, stationery required or attendance at events.
➛ *remboursé des frais engagés/de vos débours.*

However, ***we will provide a small honorarium of*** £500 at the end of your programme.
➛ *vous recevrez une prime de*

Should you have to quit before the expiry date of your contract ***a week's notice would be required***.
➛ *il vous faudrait donner une semaine de préavis.*

V. APPLICATIONS (FROM INTERNSHIPS TO PERMANENT CONTRACTS) CANDIDATURES (DU STAGE AU CDI)

a) Backing an application Appuyer une candidature

I'll do my best to open doors or ***smooth paths for you***.
➛ *aplanir les difficultés.*

I'll put a good word in for you.
➛ *Je lui adresserai un petit mot de recommandation.*

I'd be happy to forward your CV to the Human Resources Department.
➛ *Je transmettrais volontier/avec plaisir votre CV au service des Ressources Humaines.*

I'm looking forward to passing on ***your resume*** to our HR department director.
➛ *votre CV*

With more than 20 years of experience in the vaccines environment, ***this new position is a natural move consistent with Florence's background***.

➣ *ce poste représente une évolution de carrière qui correspond bien au parcours de Florence.*

We understand that ***this is a key learning opportunity for William and trust that he will be involved in the business and will acquire on-the-job-experience***.

➣ *ceci représente une occasion unique pour William, qui, nous n'en doutons pas, pourra ainsi participer à la vie de l'entreprise tout en bénéficiant d'une formation pratique.*

b) Refusing an application
Refuser une candidature

Unfortunately, we are not able to help your daughter with an assignment at Tazina & Co as ***we are in the midst of a major restructure*** at the moment.

➣ *nous sommes en pleine restructuration*

Sorry ***we have to turn down your application for an internship***. We have serious time constraints, are reducing our staff, and have our own resources to manage.

➣ *nous ne pouvons retenir votre candidature en tant que stagiaire.*

There has been a high level of interest in this post and unfortunately on this occasion you haven't been successful.

➣ *Nous avons reçu beaucoup de candidatures pour ce poste et nous ne pouvons malheureusement pas donner suite à votre demande. Cependant votre CV a retenu notre attention.*

I'm sorry to disappoint you but can I take this opportunity to thank you for taking the time and trouble to send in an application for the post?

…and wish you all the very best for the future.

c) Accepting an application
Accepter une candidature

We will be happy to welcome you as an ***intern*** during this summer period of the 16 May until the 12 August.

➛ *stagiaire*

I am sorry I did not get back to you earlier but I wanted to discuss this with a couple of managers before I gave you a final answer.

➛ *Je suis désolé(e) de ne pas être revenu(e) vers vous plus tôt/ de n'avoir pas repris contact plus tôt*

Mapping out the future

Dessiner l'avenir

I. PLANNING AHEAD PLANIFIER

"Certain matters" discussed in this presentation may constitute ***major stumbling blocks*** in future. We need to give them our full attention.

➛ *des écueils de taille/des obstacles*

We have to agree on common definitions and guidelines in order to ***gain more negotiating leverage***.

➛ *renforcer nos leviers de négociation.*

The current estimates suggest that this is ***a growth area***. Extra staff will be needed.

➛ *secteur en croissance.*

We have Key Performance Indicators to ***measure delivery against target***.

➛ *confronter les progrès réalisés avec les objectifs à atteindre.*

Thank you for your relentless hard work in achieving our short-term goals. Looking ahead, as you are aware, our company is being restructured, ***in order to meet head-on the challenges that await us***.

➛ *pour affronter les défis qui nous attendent.*

Next year, significant improvements will be made which ***will be a driving force behind our customer-focused approach***.

➛ *seront la force motrice de notre demarche qui met le client au cœur de notre action.*

Our programme will be crucial in ***enhancing our position*** as a choice partner on the market.

➛ *renforcer notre position*

Please let me know if you agree with the concept. Assuming that you do, who from our subsidiary company would you recommend we involve in the project?

➛ *Dites-moi si vous êtes d'accord avec ce concept. Partant du principe que oui*

If you notionally agree with and are broadly in line with our strategy, who from our team would it make sense to involve?

➛ *Si sur le principe vous êtes d'accord avec notre stratégie et que vous y adhérez dans les grandes lignes, qui dans l'équipe serait-il judicieux d'y associer ?*

This transition phase requires a change in mentality as well as a change in our day-to-day routine.

We have to ***address these issues***, whether they be short-term priorities or longer range strategic goals.

➛ *aborder ces questions/nous attaquer à ces enjeux*

We need ***a way to cross-check*** the current HR/R&D priorities

➛ *une façon de confronter*

Our immediate concern/most pressing need/number-one-priority ***is to establish a series of sub-goals***.

➛ *La priorité à ce stade est de définir des sous-objectifs.*

The lessons learnt in the past have now become ***a blueprint for*** the future.

➛ *canevas/cadre général*

Our strategy should be to ***lower people's expectations in the hope they'll be pleasantly surprised***.

➛ *modérer les attentes des gens pour que la surprise soit dans le bon sens/pour qu'ils soient heureusement surpris.*

The programme will run for an initial 8 weeks and may be prolonged.

➛ *La durée initialement prévue pour ce programme est de huit semaines, avec une possible prolongation.*

Perhaps we should ***think a little further ahead and allow for any slippage that may creep in.***

➛ *nous projeter en avant et garder à l'esprit qu'il peut y avoir des impondérables à prendre en compte.*

We need to ***be thinking 3 steps ahead***: what alternatives we can offer, how these can be implemented and where our subsidiary intervenes.

➛ *aborder la question en trois temps*

Unless there is joined-up thinking on this matter, the project is heading straight for disaster. ***Consistency is of the essence***.

➛ *Sans une réflexion conjointe/collective [...] Il est essentiel que nous soyons cohérents/nous devons avant tout viser la cohérence.*

Depending on the stages of the project, ***people's time commitment*** will be 30-50%.

➛ *l'investissement temps des collaborateurs*

We should move very cautiously, and NOT be ready to ***give too much away.***

➛ *faire trop de concessions/ne rien lâcher.*

Arriving a couple of days prior to the meeting ***will maximise work time efficiency, but will of course, increase travel expenses***.

➛ *permettra de travailler plus efficacement/un meilleur rendement, mais en revanche, augmentera les frais de déplacement.*

II. USING AVAILABLE RESOURCES
UTILISER LES RESSOURCES EXISTANTES

We'll need to ***allocate a large number of people*** to certain departments.

➛ *allouer plus de personnel*

We will have our staff work at optimum efficiency.

➛ *Notre priorité sera l'efficacité optimale de nos équipes.*

It will take time and numbers to see the project through.

➣ *Il faudra du temps et du personnel pour mener le projet à bien.*

External attendees have been assigned to ***each break-away group***.

➣ *petit groupe/sous groupe.*

People don't ***have a full workload***. We will have to put our heads together as to how we can maximise efficiency.

➣ *charge de travail complète.*

III. SPECULATION RÉFLÉCHIR ET ANTICIPER

This might turn out to be a complete sticking point for us. We need to be vigilant so as not to hold back the whole process.

➣ *Ceci peut se révéler être une pierre d'achoppement/un point de friction. Restons vigilants et veillons à ne pas ralentir l'ensemble du processus.*

This is unlikely to fly unless we come up with some compelling arguments.

➣ *Ceci ne tiendra pas la route à moins d'avoir des arguments en béton/vraiment convaincants.*

It will be ***an opportunity to discuss the challenges we've overcome, our successes to date and future opportunities.***

➣ *l'occasion d'évoquer les défis relevés, les points marqués et les perspectives d'avenir.*

I can foresee a few hiccups immediately after the move: why not bring the matter up for discussion at our next meeting?

➣ *Je présage/j'entrevois quelques incidents de parcours consécutifs au déménagement. Pourquoi ne pas évoquer la question à la prochaine réunion ?*

Wait and see, we may well be surprised.

➣ *Patience, attendons de voir*

••• PART THREE •••

A phrase a day

365 locutions au fil des jours

INTRODUCTION

Attending meetings and subsequently writing the minutes can be an interruption to and an imposition on an overstretched timetable. It can, however, be one of the highlights in the working lives of personal assistants, and there are those rare occasions when it gives a real sense of being privy to high-level talks. More routinely but importantly, it is a sure way of keeping in touch with the pulse of the team and their most immediate concerns; an opportunity to familiarise oneself with names, and to develop one's own mental map of all the people however remotely connected to the ongoing projects; an understanding of who does what and of the pressures brought to bear on the team as well as the deadlines they have to work to. Preparing the agenda also goes some way towards achieving this.

However personal assistants, especially those acting in a bilingual capacity, may find that taking the minutes is frustrating. Not only do they have to battle through obscure acronyms and industry-specific jargon, but they also have to adapt to the highly individual language used by some, or be attuned to accents remote from Received Pronunciation. Well-meaning team members will helpfully volunteer that only the salient points need be recorded. Yet, only knowledge based on years of experience within the same department will make it possible to distinguish what is essential from what isn't. Ongoing listening and simultaneously summarising requires seniority in the team.

I sat in on a number of meetings. They were held by experts on subjects ranging from, in no particular order, satellites and remote sensing, biotechnology, wire processing, thermostatic cartridges, HR Services and HR Solutions. All focused on high technology, and day to day matters. Each had its brand of humour – and the language to match. Within the scope of what is tonally appropriate, the spectrum of language registers is broad and escapes the strict confines of business talk. Idioms crop up, crisp and to the point. The 366 entries contained in this chapter (one for each day all year round) have been drawn from both what English and French native speakers say in the present day. They have earned their place in the lexicon of management and meeting rooms and all have their own particular flavour to which a corresponding language might not always be able to do justice. Something can often be lost in translation. Where no exact equivalent exists, attempts have been made to bring those idioms alive in the other language. Readers may browse through them for pleasure and for the sheer enjoyment of observing the words in the company they keep. They can also be more practical and use the thematic grouping in which they are presented as a guide in their search for a particular idiom.

I. ANALYSIS/POINT OF VIEW ANALYSE/POINT DE VUE

This theory has holes

This theory has holes/is flawed.

➛ *Cette théorie qui n'est pas sans faille.*

Something isn't adding up

Something isn't adding up here. The signature of the contract postdates the actual time when the consultants were in our employ.

➛ *Il y a quelque chose qui cloche : la signature du contrat est postérieure aux dates auxquelles les consultants ont travaillé pour nous.*

All else besides

I think that, all else besides, we should follow our instincts on this one.

➛ *Maintenant que nous avons passé toutes les possibilités en revue, nous devrions suivre notre instinct.*

By any measure

By any measure, the benefits outweigh the costs.

➛ *Les avantages sont incontestablement supérieurs aux inconvénients.*

A good spread of reasons

Our decision was carefully thought out and we wouldn't have signed without a good spread of reasons for accepting the deal.

➛ *Notre décision a été mûrement réfléchie et c'est parce que les raisons d'accepter le marché étaient suffisantes que nous avons signé.*

Hard-headed logic

A hard-headed logic at work!

➛ *Quelle logique imparable !*

Fair dos

Fair dos, you can't blame him for being too committed to the project, it's his baby after all.

➤ *Il faut être juste, on ne peut pas lui reprocher de trop s'investir dans le projet, c'est son bébé après tout.*

Not exactly long on

His proposal isn't exactly long on imagination.

➤ *On ne peut pas dire que sa proposition soit très originale.*

A no-brainer

Five of our team can't be in two places at once. It's a no-brainer.

➤ *Cinq membres de notre équipe ne peuvent être à deux endroits à la fois/ils n'ont pas le don d'ubiquité, c'est une évidence.*

Gossip

This is just gossip that passes for analysis.

➤ *Ce sont seulement des commérages/ce sont seulement des bruits de couloir qui font office d'analyses.*

The argument is weak

The argument is weak and will easily be dismissed as implausible.

➤ *L'argument ne tient pas la route. Les gens le rejetteront comme étant peu plausible.*

The sub-text I'm reading

The sub-text I'm reading here is that the appointed coordinator didn't do his job properly.

➤ *Ce qui pour moi ressort en filigrane dans ce que vous dites, c'est que le coordinateur attitré/que nous avions nommé n'a pas fait son travail correctement.*

A whole set of circumstances

Not just one thing contributed to the mixed results, but a whole set of circumstances.

➤ *C'est tout un ensemble qui a conduit à ce bilan mitigé, pas seulement un élément.*

It wouldn't look good, would it?

It wouldn't look good if we came into the meeting in dribs and drabs, would it?

➛ *Ça ne ferait pas sérieux si nous nous entrions en réunion les uns après les autres/en petits groupes.*

Horses for courses

Consultants did brilliantly on our Comp and Ben study, but would they be as good on a Performance project? It's a case of "horses for courses".

➛ *A chacun ses compétences. Nos consultants ont été excellents sur le dossier Comp and Ben ; est-ce que cela veut dire qu'ils le seraient également pour le projet Performance ?*

II. ARGUING THE CASE ARGUMENTATION

Prove conclusively

He made the case that proved conclusively that the guidelines were self-defeating.

➛ *Il a démontré par A + B que les directives allaient à l'encontre du but recherché.*

Embrace a cliché

Call me unafraid to embrace a cliché, but Economics is also known as the "dismal science", isn't it?

➛ *Peut-être me jugerez-vous audacieux de cautionner un lieu commun, mais l'économie n'est-elle pas également connue sous le nom de « science funeste » ?*

Despite protestations to the contrary

Despite protestations to the contrary they did little to promote the project in front of the CEO.

➛ *Bien qu'ils s'en défendent, ils ont très peu travaillé pour promouvoir le projet auprès du Directeur Général.*

Above and beyond the fact that

Above and beyond the fact that the candidate ticks all the boxes, her academic record is outstanding and this can only be a plus.

➣ *Au-delà du fait que la candidate correspond en tout point au profil demandé, son itinéraire universitaire est remarquable et cela ne peut que jouer en sa faveur.*

A moot point

Whether the plan will outlive its architect/creator after he's left the company, is a moot point.

➣ *On est en droit de se demander si le plan survivra à son auteur après son départ de la société.*

Here I rest my case

The figures say it all. Here I rest my case.

➣ *Pas besoin d'ajouter quoi que ce soit, les chiffres parlent d'eux-mêmes/CQFD.*

III. CLEARSIGHTEDNESS CLAIRVOYANCE

Right on the money

I thought his visit was more than a courtesy call and I was right on the money!

➣ *Je pensais bien que sa visite n'était pas une simple visite de courtoisie, et j'avais tout bon/j'ai tapé dans le mille !*

With all the potential for

With all the potential for misunderstanding and misinterpretation.

➣ *Avec tous les risques de malentendu ou de confusion que cela comporte.*

A wider set of issues

You need to look at the broader picture and take into account a wider set of issues.

➣ *Il faut voir la situation dans son ensemble et remettre cela dans son contexte.*

A cautionary tale

The contract nearly fell through because of a procedural technicality. This is a cautionary tale for the future.

➣ *Nous avons failli perdre le contrat à cause d'un vice de forme. Nous devons en tirer un enseignement pour l'avenir.*

The tale holds several lessons

It's been a long saga of failed partnerships with leading companies, but the tale holds several lessons for us.

➣ *Nos interminables tentatives de partenariats avec des entreprises de renom ont certes échoué, mais nous avons plusieurs enseignements à tirer de cette expérience.*

It should hold up

As it is the project should hold up/should be viable. Its aims are threefold.

➣ *Tel quel, le projet devrait tenir la route. Son objectif est triple.*

A few removes from

We are a few removes from the next major stage in our project and the outlook is good.

➣ *Nous approchons d'une nouvelle étape importante de notre projet et nous sommes confiants dans nos chances de succès/et les pronostics sont bons.*

It isn't fanciful to think that

It isn't fanciful to think that after the go-live, our workload will be greatly reduced.

➣ *Il n'est pas déraisonnable de dire que/on peut raisonnablement penser qu'une fois le lancement terminé, notre charge de travail sera considérablement allégée.*

You can see that with half an eye

They are playing for time. You can see that with half an eye.

➣ *Ils essaient de gagner du temps. Cela saute aux yeux/c'est une évidence.*

Have the potential to

This scheme has the potential to reap us some very handsome profits over the foreseeable future.

➛ *Voici un plan susceptible de nous faire réaliser des bénéfices non négligeables à l'avenir.*

Staying power

Endurance

I. PERSISTENCE **TÉNACITÉ**

Keep your nose to the grindstone

We're keeping our noses to the grindstone. We've got to work to punishing deadlines.

➛ *On a le nez dans le guidon en ce moment. Les délais sont très serrés/on en bave avec les délais.*

Against all odds

Against all odds, we met the deadlines.

➛ *Contre toute attente/bien que tout ait été contre nous, nous avons réussi à tenir les délais.*

Come hell or high water

Once we have drawn up our budget for next year, we have to be prepared to stick up for it come hell or high water.

➛ *Une fois que nous nous serons entendus sur le budget de l'année prochaine nous devons être prêts à le défendre contre vents et marées.*

Burn rubber

Three weeks to organise the seminar? We'll have to burn rubber on this one.

➛ *Comment ? Trois semaines pour organiser le séminaire ? Il va falloir mettre la gomme/il ne va pas falloir chômer.*

Clear the decks

Once the first stage has been reached, we'll clear the decks for Stage two.

➛ *Une fois la phase 1 terminée, nous pourrons mettre le paquet sur la phase 2/branle-bas de combat pour la phase 2 !*

Like drawing teeth

Getting the information was like drawing teeth, they are very secretive about their research programme.

➛ *Ça a été la croix et la bannière pour obtenir ces informations. Ils font grand mystère de leur programme de recherche.*

Get out there

Well, there's no point in sitting and watching. We'll have to get out there and do what's to be done.

➛ *Rien ne sert de rester à regarder sans rien faire, il faut aller au charbon/mieux vaut passer à l'action.*

Work at the coal face

People at the top have no idea what people working at the coal face like us do.

➛ *Les gens dans les hautes sphères ne se rendent pas compte de ce que c'est que d'aller au charbon comme nous le faisons/ de mouiller sa chemise.*

Get down and dirty

The computer developers are the ones who both get down and dirty and get the blame when things go wrong.

➛ *Ce sont les informaticiens qui vont au charbon/qui mettent les mains dans le cambouis, et qui de surcroît se font taper sur les doigts quand quelque chose ne va pas.*

Slaving away

We owe the essential work to the people slaving away in the boiler room.

➛ *Nous sommes redevables du plus gros du travail à ceux qui vont au charbon/qui triment en soute.*

It goes with the territory

Sometimes being a senior manager means you have to make unpopular decisions; it goes with the territory.

➛ *Être cadre de direction signifie parfois que l'on doit prendre des décisions impopulaires. Ca fait partie du boulot/c'est la fonction qui veut ça.*

Time to get stuck in

Get out there and do what's got to be done/Now it's time to get stuck in/Now it's time to get cracking.

➛ *Il faut aller au charbon.*

At the sharp end

Our computer engineers are at the sharp end of Enterprise Application Software; they know exactly what "living life on the edge" means!

➛ *Les informaticiens sont en première ligne de l'activité Solutions d'entreprise ; ils savent fort bien ce que signifie « être sur le fil du rasoir ».*

The school of hard knocks

He eventually got to the top through the school of hard knocks/only by learning the hard way.

➛ *Il est arrivé en haut de l'échelle, mais il a été à dure école.*

A job and a half

That's a job and a half, isn't it?

➛ *Ce n'est pas une sinécure !*

We've got our work cut out

We've got our work cut out for us, so let's get cracking!

➛ *Nous avons du pain sur la planche, alors allons-y !*

Work flat out

The deadline is approaching and we are working flat out/working our socks off.

➛ *L'échéance arrive et on est au taquet/on travaille d'arrache-pied.*

II. PRESSURE PRESSION

A marathon task

It's a marathon task.

➛ *C'est une course contre la montre/c'est un vrai marathon.*

At a moment's notice

I had to give them a rundown on the scope of our project-related activities at a moment's notice. Good job I had this summary chart at the ready/to hand/handy.

➛ *J'ai dû leur présenter au pied levé l'ensemble de nos activités liées au projet. J'étais bien content(e) d'avoir ce récapitulatif sous le coude.*

Sustain the pace

Yes, but can the team sustain the pace? It seems we've reached breaking point already.

➛ *L'équipe peut-elle tenir le rythme ? Nous sommes déjà à bout.*

Thrive under pressure

I don't think the team would thrive under pressure.

➛ *Je ne pense pas que travailler sous pression serait bénéfique à l'équipe.*

In complete meltdown

On the day of the go-live, the sudden increase in traffic made the system crash. The office was in complete meltdown!

➛ *Le jour du Go Live, un goulot d'étranglement a entraîné l'effondrement du système. C'était la panique au bureau.*

A few sticky moments

We had a few sticky moments mostly involving the no-show of a key guest, a bad connection with the US and two faulty mikes…

➛ *Nous avons eu quelques sueurs froides dues, pour résumer, à l'absence d'un intervenant clé, à une mauvaise liaison avec les US et à deux micros muets.*

Chart a steady course

The select group working on the programme have charted a steady course through the whirl of activity, the red alerts and pressures galore.

➛ *Le petit groupe chargé de ce programme ne s'est pas laissé détourner de ses objectifs/est resté imperturbable malgré le tourbillon d'activités, les alertes rouges et pressions en tous genres.*

Step up to the plate

If things get difficult, we'll have to react quickly and step up to the plate.

➣ *En cas de difficulté, il nous faudra réagir rapidement et répondre présent/être sur le pont/être au taquet.*

She ran herself into the ground

She ran herself into the ground jetting around the world.

➣ *Elle s'est épuisée à passer sa vie dans les avions et parcourir le monde.*

Hit the ground running

I hit the ground running this morning and have worked flat out since.

➣ *J'ai commencé la journée sur les chapeaux de roues et je n'ai pas arrêté depuis.*

At full capacity

There's no way we can take on any more commitments, we're at full capacity/we've reached saturation point/the cup is full.

➣ *Nous ne pouvons pas nous rajouter du travail, on est au taquet déjà/ nous fonctionnons à plein rendement.*

Time sensitive

Not an emergency, just time sensitive. There's no time to lose.

➣ *Ce n'est pas urgent ; simplement le temps est un facteur déterminant. Activons-nous !*

Clearsightedness

Prévoyance

I. DIRECTION **MAINTENIR LE CAP**

Don't go there!

I'm in charge of tracking down damaged spare parts sent back for repair. It's a nightmare, don't go there!

➛ *J'assure le suivi des pièces de rechange endommagées que l'on renvoie pour réparation. C'est une véritable usine à gaz.*

In for the long haul

Once you get involved in the spare parts department, you're in for the long haul.

➛ *Une fois que tu commences à t'occuper des pièces détachées, tu verras, c'est une vraie usine à gaz.*

Get one's bearings

It is almost impossible to get one's bearings in such a maze of rules and regulations.

➛ *Il est pratiquement impossible de se repérer dans ce dédale juridique.*

Let's not be led away from

Let's remember this is our number one priority. Let's not be led away from our goals at this stage.

➛ *N'oublions pas que ceci est notre priorité numéro un. Ne nous laissons pas détourner de nos objectifs.*

A ringside seat

She's a living embodiment of the company's history, having had a ringside seat throughout its entire development.

➛ *Elle est la mémoire vivante de notre entreprise. Elle a été aux premières loges pour tous les évènements critiques qui ont marqué son évolution.*

The decider

The candidate had had working experience in Asia before, and that was the decider.

➛ *Le candidat avait travaillé en Asie, c'est cela qui a été le facteur décisif.*

Find my way around

I'm beginning to find my way around the accounts.

➛ *Je commence à mieux m'y retrouver dans les comptes.*

Get our marching orders

Well, we've got our marching orders which are to power ahead against all odds.

➛ *Nous avons le mot d'ordre/les instructions : foncer quoiqu'il arrive/avancer envers et contre tout.*

Bend with the wind

We can't come up with any definite proposals because at the moment we've no idea what the top management's guidelines are going to be. So at the meeting, let's just bend with the wind.

➛ *A ce stade, il nous est impossible de faire une proposition, puisque nous n'avons reçu aucune directive d'en haut. A la prochaine réunion nous n'aurons qu'à aller dans le sens du vent.*

II. REALISM RÉALISME

A fool's paradise

If you think further discussions unnecessary for the project's go-ahead, you're living in a fool's paradise.

➛ *Si vous pensez obtenir la validation du projet sans davantage de discussions, vous vous bercez d'illusions.*

Not by a long chalk!

We're nowhere near meeting the deadlines. Not by a long chalk!

➛ *Nous ne sommes pas près de tenir les délais, loin s'en faut.*

Way off the mark

We need the exact figures here; otherwise we'll end up way off the mark.

➛ *Tenons-nous en aux chiffres exacts, ce serait facile d'être complètement à côté de la plaque dans nos estimations.*

Off-beam

We could easily go completely off-beam, so let's get our data right.

➛ *On peut facilement être à côté de la plaque, mieux vaut s'assurer que nos données sont bonnes.*

Wide of the mark

Their forecast is wide of the mark: judging from the current headcount, we'll need at least two more FTEs in the coming months.

➛ *Ils sont loin du compte dans leurs prévisions : au vu des effectifs actuels, ce sont deux intérimaires supplémentaires dont nous aurons besoin dans les mois à venir.*

Completely out of it

Whenever we start discussing our sales plan for the next two years, it's clear that he's completely out of it/he hasn't got a clue what we're talking about.

➛ *Dès que nous commençons à discuter de notre plan commercial pour les deux années à venir, on voit bien qu'il n'est pas dans le coup/qu'il est complètement à côté.*

Magic out of thin air

We can't magic two FTEs out of thin air. On top of the management's approval for this, we need time.

➛ *On n'aura pas deux salariés en claquant des doigts. En plus de l'aval de la direction, c'est de temps dont nous aurons besoin.*

More fool them!

If they think this will actually develop customer loyalty, well more fool them!

➛ *S'ils pensent qu'ils vont fidéliser le client comme ça, ils se mettent le doigt dans l'œil.*

III. WISDOM SAGESSE

Meet trouble half way

Let's not meet trouble half way/put ourselves in harm's way and make sure we carry out the normal procedure.

➣ *N'allons pas au devant des difficultés, et suivons la procédure normale.*

Better ask a silly question

Better ask a silly question than make a silly mistake.

➣ *Mieux vaut poser une question stupide que de stupidement se planter.*

Raise our sights

Let's not admit defeat and raise our sights to focus on what we can achieve within the limited timeframe.

➣ *Ne nous avouons pas vaincus. Voyons plus loin et concentrons-nous plutôt sur ce qu'il nous est possible de réussir dans le peu de temps imparti.*

Discretion is the better part of valour

We have a potentially explosive situation here, so we have to be sensible and avoid sparking off a crisis. Discretion is the better part of valour.

➣ *Nous avons à faire à une situation explosive. Soyons vigilants et évitons de déclencher une crise. Prudence est mère de sûreté.*

Let's not get ahead of ourselves

We have a full order book for the coming year, but let's not get ahead of ourselves and let's not think of expanding right now.

➣ *Notre carnet de commandes est rempli pour cette année. Ceci dit, restons calmes/pas de précipitation, nous développer n'est pas à l'ordre du jour.*

Win some, lose some

The deal was well under way, almost sure to result in a contract. Nothing came of it though. Oh, well, win some, lose some.

➣ *L'affaire était bien engagée et allait à coup sûr déboucher. Mais non, rien ne s'est concrétisé : on ne peut pas gagner à tous les coups.*

Don't close off all your options

Make sure that you don't antagonize Human Resources when negotiating the terms of your departure. Don't close off all your options.

➛ *Veille à ne pas te mettre les ressources humaines à dos au moment de négocier ton départ. Garde-toi des cartouches/ne te ferme pas toutes les portes.*

While the going is good

With the forthcoming cuts, holiday benefits are bound to be affected, so we'd better start looking into possible company holiday packages while the going is good.

➛ *Au vu des compressions budgétaires, le budget vacances va pâtir. Nous devrions profiter de commencer à prospecter les possibilités d'un voyage avec le comité d'entreprise pendant qu'il en est encore temps.*

A word of caution

I would just like to add a word of caution here. Given the preparations needed for a seminar on that scale, we'll need at least 2 months' notice.

➛ *Petite mise en garde : vu les préparatifs que va demander un séminaire de cette envergure, il nous faut le prévoir au moins deux mois à l'avance.*

Two heads are better than one

Two heads are better than one, as they say, so let's get together and see what we can come up with.

➛ *Plusieurs avis valent mieux qu'un/Il y en a toujours plus dans deux têtes que dans une. Réfléchissons et voyons ce qu'il en ressortira.*

Nothing ventured, nothing gained

I know this is a bit risky, but nothing ventured, nothing gained.

➛ *Je sais bien que c'est un peu risqué mais qui ne tente rien n'a rien.*

Time will prove them right or wrong

At this particular juncture, it is difficult to say if their decision is wise. Time will prove them right or wrong.

➛ *A ce stade, il est difficile de dire si leur décision est sage. C'est le temps qui leur donnera raison ou tort.*

Don't spoil the ship for a ha'porth of tar

We've made a great job of a mammoth task, so let's not spoil the ship for a ha'porth of tar [half a penny worth of tar].

➛ *Nous avons fait un travail colossal. Ne risquons pas de tout compromettre en voulant économiser trois francs six sous.*

Slow and steady wins the race

If we proceed methodically, we'll get there in good time. Slow and steady wins the race.

➛ *Si nous procédons méthodiquement et que nous nous en tenons à nos objectifs, nous y arriverons en temps. Rien ne sert de courir.*

Taking a stance

Prendre parti

I. APPROVAL/SUPPORT APPROBATION/SOUTIEN

I'm behind you

Whatever you decide, I'm behind you all the way.

➛ *Quelle que soit votre décision, vous pouvez absolument compter sur moi/je vous suis à 100 %/je suis à fond derrière vous.*

Supporting us to the hilt

I'm pleased to announce that we got Amanda's stamp of approval. In fact, she's supporting us to the hilt.

➛ *Je suis ravi de vous annoncer qu'Amanda nous a donné le feu vert. En fait, elle nous soutient à fond.*

Seal of approval

I'm right behind you. You have got my complete seal of approval.

➛ *Je vous suis là-dessus. Vous avez mon entière approbation.*

Chime in with

I took it on me to say that our policy is more about progressive improvement than drastic reforms. Would you chime in with that?

➛ *J'ai pris sur moi de dire que notre politique était davantage progressiste que réformiste. Tu me rejoins là-dessus ?/C'est comme ça que tu vois les choses toi aussi ?*

I'll key in to

I'll key in to what has just been said, by adding that some of our resources have been earmarked to deal with this issue.

➛ *Je voudrais renchérir sur ce qui vient d'être dit en précisant que des ressources ont été affectées à ce projet.*

She rubberstamped the deal

She rubberstamped the deal but it doesn't reflect her usual scrupulousness.

➛ *Elle a approuvé l'accord sans discussion, ce qui ne correspond pas à son naturel habituellement très pointilleux.*

Proponents and critics

Proponents of this policy argue that it would drive down costs; critics say it would affect quality.

➛ *Les partisans de cette politique considèrent qu'elle réduirait les coûts ; ses détracteurs, quant à eux, y voient une menace pour la qualité.*

To be sold on

They are completely sold on these two ideas.

➛ *Ils sont devenus inconditionnels de ces deux idées.*

Buy in to

The seminar marked a turning point; the delegates bought in to two main ideas and their commitment will be instrumental in carrying the project through.

➛ *Le séminaire a marqué un tournant. Les participants nous ont rejoints sur deux idées force et leur concours sera déterminant pour la réalisation de notre projet.*

Non-committal

When asked about the future of the lay-off plan, she remained non-committal.

➛ *Lorsqu'on l'a interrogée sur la question des plans de licenciements, elle est restée très évasive.*

Come down strongly for

At the board of directors, the Managing Director came down strongly for my three point plan.

➛ *Au comité de direction, le PDG s'est prononcé fortement en faveur de mon plan en trois volets.*

II. CONFLICT/OPPOSITION/CRITICISM — CONFLIT/OPPOSITION/CRITIQUE

Fan the flames of

You don't want to be fanning the flames of a debate that's been smouldering.

➣ *Il vaut mieux éviter de relancer une controverse larvée.*

A trenchant critic of

He's a trenchant critic of the company's restructuring programme (clear, effective and forceful).

➣ *C'est un virulent détracteur de la politique de restructuration menée par l'entreprise.*

Hare-brained policies

I can't believe they're endorsing hare-brained policies like this one!

➣ *Je n'arrive pas à comprendre comment ils cautionnent des mesures aussi loufoques que ça.*

Fight one's corner

Everyone's fighting his/her corner and looking after individual interests.

➣ *Chacun défend ses positions et voit son propre intérêt.*

A divisive issue

The decision to move the headquarters hundreds of miles away is a divisive issue.

➣ *Une question propre à semer la discorde/semer la zizanie.*

Constant carping

This won't spare us having to answer clients' constant carping.

➣ *Cela ne nous épargnera pas les incessantes doléances des clients.*

The nay-sayers

Our success has proved the nay-sayers wrong.

➣ *Notre succès a donné tort aux sceptiques.*

Don't start any fires!

The possibility that there may be lay-offs is less than remote, but let's not talk about it at this stage. We don't want to start any fires!

➛ *Je sais qu'il y a de sérieux risques de licenciements, mais n'en disons rien dans l'immédiat. N'échauffons pas les esprits !/Ne mettons pas le feu aux poudres !*

Knock an idea on the head

The idea needs to be knocked on the head.

➛ *Il faut faire un sort à/en finir avec cette idée.*

Take the flak

We take the flak if the deadlines are not met.

➛ *Nous nous faisons descendre en flammes si les échéances ne sont pas respectées.*

To lay into

No work will ever get done if they keep laying into us about our modus operandi.

➛ *Nous n'avancerons jamais s'ils n'arrêtent pas de tirer à boulets rouges sur nous/critiquer nos méthodes.*

Go up in arms

The closing of the site came as a blow to the company's employees. The staff representative went up in arms, and leapt to the defence of those who were hardest hit.

➛ *La fermeture du site a porté un coup aux salariés. Le représentant du personnel est monté au créneau et a pris la défense des plus touchés par cette mesure.*

III. RIGIDITY INFLEXIBILITÉ

On a wholesale basis

Should we refuse any dealings with them on a wholesale basis?

➛ *Devrions-nous refuser en bloc toute transaction avec eux ?*

IV. UNCERTAINTY INCERTITUDE

Go down to the wire

Persuading them to put up more money for the project was never going to be easy, and it really went down to the wire, didn't it?

➛ *Les convaincre de consentir plus de fonds pour le projet n'était pas gagné d'avance : c'est resté incertain jusqu'au dernier moment.*

The wild card

The wild card for the Go Live is how many people will be trying to log on at exactly the same time.

➛ *L'impondérable/ce qui peut changer la donne pour le lancement du logiciel, c'est le nombre d'utilisateurs qui vont tenter de se connecter au même moment.*

The jury is out

I'm not sure we should release the information now. The jury is out on that.

➛ *Vaut-il mieux divulguer l'information tout de suite ? La question n'est pas encore tranchée/cela reste à voir.*

On a knife-edge

Negotiations for our site to remain open are going full swing/are going hard and strong, but the outcome remains on a knife-edge.

➛ *Les négociations contre la fermeture de notre site battent leur plein, mais l'issue reste incertaine.*

I don't have a line on

I don't have a line on what's going to happen.

➛ *Je n'ai aucune idée de ce qui va se passer*

It's touch and go

It's touch and go whether we'll get all the survey's responses in time.

➛ *Récupérer à temps toutes les réponses à l'enquête, ce n'est pas gagné d'avance/c'est quitte ou double.*

Strategy

Stratégie

I. MEDIUM AND LONG-TERM PLANNING
PLANIFIER SUR LE LONG-MOYEN TERME

Drive up quality, drive down cost

Drive up quality, drive down cost that's our motto.

➛ *Améliorer la qualité et réduire les coûts telle est notre devise.*

The thrust

The proposals are a bit short on detail, but the thrust is correct.

➛ *Les propositions gagneraient à être plus détaillées, mais elles vont dans le bon sens/l'esprit y est.*

More riding on this

They have more riding on this than we do.

➛ *Là-dessus, leurs enjeux sont plus importants que les nôtres.*

A lot riding on

There's a lot riding on the outcome of the talks.

➛ *De l'issue des pourparlers dépendent beaucoup de choses.*

Guard against all eventualities

We should guard against all eventualities; otherwise we're in for a hard landing.

➛ *Si nous ne parons pas à toute éventualité, l'atterrissage va être rude.*

Interim measures

Interim, short-term measures have been put into place.

➛ *Des mesures très provisoires et à court terme ont été mises en place.*

Just-in-time

Once more, we'll run on a just-in-time principle, and struggle to get the job done to meet their deadline.

➛ *Une fois de plus nous allons devoir travailler en flux tendu et nous battre/galérer pour respecter leur délai.*

Mileage

There might be some mileage in this policy.

➛ *C'est une politique qui semble avoir de l'avenir/qui fera du chemin.*

Go part of the way towards

These measures go only part of the way towards dealing with the severance package issue.

➛ *Ces mesures ne résolvent/ne règlent que partiellement la question des indemnités de licenciement.*

Wriggle room

If they are slashing our budget, we aren't going to have much leeway/wriggle room to hire new consultants, are we?

➛ *S'ils font des coupes sombres dans notre budget, nous n'aurons pas beaucoup de marge pour embaucher de nouveaux consultants.*

New zip

This should give the project new zip.

➛ *Cela devrait donner un regain d'énergie au projet.*

A backup plan

You can't just resign and walk straight into a new job. You need a backup plan/a contingency plan.

➛ *C'est illusoire de penser que tu peux donner ta démission et trouver un emploi dans la foulée. Il te faut un plan B.*

Play our cards right

If we play our cards right, we'll have done the deal before end of year.

➛ *Si nous la jouons fine/si nous naviguons bien, nous aurons conclu le marché avant la fin de l'année.*

Whether by accident or design

Whether by accident or design the CEO got wind of his right hand man's scheming and he appointed him to office abroad.

➛ *Était-ce par hasard ou à dessein, mais le PDG a eu vent des manigances de son bras droit et l'a installé dans de nouvelles fonctions à l'étranger.*

Stake out ground

We will be staking out ground ahead of the summit.

➛ *À nous de délimiter notre champ d'action/de définir nos objectifs en vue du sommet.*

Steer the ship

Someone's got to steer the ship.

➛ *Il faut bien qu'il y ait quelqu'un aux commandes.*

An important plank

An important plank in our company policy is its commitment to equal opportunities with regards to disability.

➛ *Un point clé de la politique de recrutement de l'entreprise est sa mobilisation pour l'emploi de personnes handicapées.*

Cohere into

None of this has cohered into a clear vision for the next two years.

➛ *Tout cela est trop confus pour permettre de dégager une vision claire des deux années à venir.*

The brains behind the project

Although she isn't in the spotlight, she's the brains behind the project.

➛ *Elle n'est pas mise en avant/on ne l'a pas mise sous les feux de la rampe, mais c'est elle l'instigatrice du projet.*

Reinforces its claim on the future

With this key milestone successfully reached, our project reinforces its claim on the future.

➛ *Ce premier succès fait de notre projet un outil d'avenir.*

To kitchen sink

A new chief executive arrives and kitchen sinks all the bad news.

➛ *Un nouveau directeur arrive et met toutes les mauvaises nouvelles au panier.*

Play a waiting game

So far they've been rather quiet about the issue; they might well be playing a waiting game in the hope that we act first.

➛ *On les a peu entendus sur la question ; ce serait bien de l'attentisme de leur part pour nous laisser agir les premiers.*

Bide your time

Don't make a hasty decision. Bide your time.

➛ *Ne prenez pas de décision hâtive. Le moment viendra/sachez attendre votre heure.*

Set out a road map

It is important to set out a road map.

➛ *Il est important d'établir une feuille de route.*

At the helm

We felt totally confident that there was somebody at the helm/ on the bridge.

➛ *Nous avions la certitude que quelqu'un était à la barre/aux commandes.*

The rights and wrongs

We have to know the rights and wrongs of the scheme, before we give it a go.

➛ *Il nous faut connaitre les tenants et les aboutissants du plan, avant de nous lancer.*

Farm out

They've farmed out their computer support to a call centre outside of the company.

➛ *Ils ont sous-traité leur assistance informatique à un centre d'appel en dehors de la société.*

Working in harness with

We are working in harness with a trusted consulting company and our partnership goes back a long way.

➛ *Actuellement nous travaillons en tandem avec une société de consultants de confiance et notre partenariat remonte à des années.*

Cut losses

He's the new man. The management decided to cut their losses and appointed him to replace Sian as project manager.

➛ *C'est lui la nouvelle recrue. La direction a décidé de limiter les dégâts et l'a nommé chef de projet en remplacement de Sian.*

A game changer

His appointment at the head of the department is a real game changer.

➛ *Sa nomination à la tête du service change la donne.*

Trim our sails

If we want to ride out the crisis, we'll have to trim our sails.

➛ *Si nous voulons sortir de la crise, il faudra voir d'où vient le vent et agir en conséquence.*

Being methodical

Méthode

I. SHORT-TERM PLANNING | PLANIFIER SUR LE COURT TERME

Put their house in order

They are hardly in a position to lecture us. They'd better put their house in order first/clean up their own backyard first.

➣ *Qui sont-ils pour nous donner des leçons ? Ils feraient mieux de balayer devant leur porte.*

Puzzle out the details

Let's look at the bigger picture first and puzzle out the details later.

➣ *Voyons la situation dans son ensemble dans un premier temps. Nous règlerons les détails/démêlerons les détails plus tard.*

Throw something together

He said that in order to hand in the report on time, he'd have to throw something together.

➣ *Il a dit que pour rendre son rapport en temps et en heure, il lui faudrait improviser quelque chose à la hâte/le bâcler/le faire à la six-quatre-deux.*

Reframe the debate

We'll have to reframe the debate in terms of how we can protect our industry from international competition.

➣ *Il va nous falloir recadrer le débat sur les moyens de protéger notre industrie de la concurrence internationale.*

Monitor progress

We'll be able to systematically monitor progress against the plan.

➣ *Nous pourrons vérifier systématiquement l'adéquation entre l'état d'avancement du projet et le planning.*

Far down the line

It's Tuesday now, so given that we've got to complete this by Friday, how far down the line are we?

➛ *Nous sommes aujourd'hui mardi ; vendredi étant notre date butoir, où en sommes-nous/où en est-on ?*

Sticking points

Write down some of your sticking points. We'll deal with them in due course.

➛ *Relevez les points de désaccord/questions litigieuses. Nous y reviendrons en temps utile.*

In the light of

We need to examine the scheme in the light of these game changing ideas.

➛ *Il nous faut revoir le plan à la lumière de ces idées neuves qui changent la donne.*

As they come

I'll be giving more details as they come.

➛ *J'apporterai des détails/je préciserai, au fur et à mesure.*

Put together

We'll put together a detailed proposal and send it to you in due course.

➛ *Nous élaborerons une proposition détaillée et nous vous l'enverrons en temps et en lieu.*

A test case

This will make it a test case for the future.

➛ *Cela en fera un cas de jurisprudence.*

A standard by which

This proposal has set a standard by which all others will be judged.

➛ *Cette proposition sera un critère de référence/servira d'étalon pour toutes les suivantes.*

A benchmark

Today's decision will serve as a benchmark for similar scenarios in future.

➛ *La décision d'aujourd'hui servira de référence dans des cas semblables à l'avenir.*

Go slow on

It is a complex issue, so we're going to go slow on this one.

➛ *La question est complexe, évitons donc la précipitation.*

Play to our strengths

Let's play to our strengths here; that will keep competition at bay.

➛ *Ce qu'il faut c'est miser sur nos points forts/rester dans notre domaine d'expertise : ça tiendra la concurrence à distance.*

To separate cause from effect

The reshuffle resulted in a strike; the strike didn't lead to the reshuffle. One has to separate cause from effect.

➛ *La réorganisation a provoqué une grève ; ce n'est pas la grève qui a entraîné la réorganisation. Il convient de distinguer la cause de l'effet.*

Trace the history

In order to understand why, let's trace the history.

➛ *Pour comprendre pourquoi, reprenons les faits.*

Oil the wheels

A team coordinator will help oil the wheels of communication.

➛ *Un coordinateur mettra un peu d'huile dans les rouages et facilitera la communication.*

A Band Aid approach

I'm not sure I like the idea of hiring a temp for the job; it strikes me as being a Band Aid approach to the problem when what we need are long-term solutions.

➛ *L'idée d'embaucher un intérimaire ne me convient pas ; c'est, me semble-t-il, une politique de pis-aller/un expédient là où nous recherchons des solutions durables.*

Shoot your bolt

Don't discuss the content of your speech before the meeting, or you may shoot your bolt.

➛ *Ne faites aucune allusion à ce qui est dit dans votre discours avant la réunion, vous risquez de jouer votre meilleur atout.*

Airbrush

There is no call for drastic changes to the policy, but it needs to be airbrushed to be perfectly in tune with the company's cuts in travel budget.

➛ *Il n'y a pas lieu de changer cette mesure de façon radicale ; il faut juste l'actualiser pour qu'elle soit en accord avec les récentes restrictions budgétaires que l'entreprise pratique sur les voyages.*

Mere tokenism

It is difficult to see this move as anything other than mere tokenism/merely tokenistic.

➛ *Il est difficile de ne pas voir dans cette initiative autre chose qu'une démarche purement formelle/pour la forme.*

To push hard into the background

These issues have been pushed hard into the background. It is high time they took their rightful place again.

➛ *Ces questions ont été reléguées au second plan. Il est grand temps qu'elles retrouvent la place qui leur revient.*

Put on hold

These are issues that will have to be put on hold for the time being.

➛ *Ce sont des questions qu'il va nous falloir mettre entre parenthèses/en attente pendant quelque temps.*

Flag it up

There are still a few inconsistencies in the document as it stands, and I thought it really important to flag that up.

➛ *Il existe encore quelques incohérences dans le document tel qu'il se présente et j'ai pensé qu'attirer l'attention là-dessus/le signaler avait son importance.*

Play hardball

If this can't be resolved through negotiation, we'll have to play hard ball with them and get tough.

➛ *Si rien ne se résout par la voie de la négociation, il va nous falloir employer la manière forte.*

Hedge our bets

This is bound to detonate a chain reaction. I suggest hedging our bets and avoid any commitment at this stage.

➛ *Cela va immanquablement déclencher une réaction en chaîne. Je propose de nous couvrir et de garder profil bas pour l'instant.*

Soft pedal it

We'll have to soft pedal it for a while; otherwise the team will never take the stress.

➛ *Il va falloir mettre la pédale douce, sinon l'équipe ne va pas tenir la longueur.*

On top of our brief

At our keynote presentation in Barcelona, we need to be completely on top of our brief.

➛ *Lors de notre présentation-programme à Barcelone, il nous faut vraiment maîtriser les moindres détails/il nous faut être au top/ connaître notre dossier à fond.*

On the back burner

We all agree that the project has a lot going for itself, but the Vice President wants to put it on the back burner.

➛ *Nous sommes tous d'accord sur les vertus du projet, mais le Vice Président a décidé de le mettre en attente/en veilleuse.*

Taking stock

Bilans

I. FACTS CONSTATS

A statement of facts

I'm not being critical here. It's only a statement of facts.

➛ *Ce n'est pas une critique. C'est seulement un constat.*

An acknowledgement of failure

Their silence on the subject amounted to an acknowledgement of failure.

➛ *Leur silence signait leur échec/était un constat d'échec.*

Post good results

The company posted good results, and we see this as a promising sign for the future.

➛ *La société a affiché de bons résultats, et nous y voyons un signe encourageant pour l'avenir.*

Cheese paring

This is a textbook case/a classic example of how budget restrictions turn out to be nothing more than cheese paring.

➛ *C'est un parfait cas d'école : ce qui passe pour restriction budgétaire n'est autre qu'une économie de bouts de chandelles.*

A bit of a curate's egg

The deal he landed is a bit of a curate's egg.

➛ *Le bilan sur le contrat qu'il a décroché est contrasté (par certains côtés il est prometteur, mais certains termes sont inacceptables).*

A far remove from

In the light of all the difficulties, we can congratulate ourselves on having come this far, but it's a far remove from what had been planned initially.

➛ *Au vu des difficultés rencontrées, nous pouvons nous féliciter du chemin parcouru, mais nous sommes bien loin de l'objectif de départ.*

Sit in on

She sat in on the committee, and observed the proceedings. She wasn't a member.

➢ *Elle assistait au comité, mais n'en était pas membre.*

Milestone

We have reached a psychologically significant 6,000 hits. Quite a milestone!

➢ *Nous avons franchi le seuil psychologique des 6 000 connexions. C'est un jalon significatif/une étape importante.*

As good as it gets

We can't offer our employees more than three weeks paid leave per annum. That's as good as it gets, I'm afraid.

➢ *Je n'ai rien d'autre à offrir à nos employés que trois semaines de congés payés annuels. On ne peut pas faire mieux/pas trouver mieux.*

We got a run for our money

We got a run for our money. The social media conference featured a panel of outstanding speakers.

➢ *Nous en avons eu pour notre argent. La conférence sur les médias sociaux rassemblait des intervenants remarquables.*

II. FIGURES CALCULS

The all-in price

The all-in price comes out at £ 4,568.

➢ *Tout compris cela revient à 5 382 €.*

Put a cap on

We can't send out the invitation to the whole department. We must put a cap on numbers.

➢ *On ne peut pas envoyer l'invitation à tout le service. Il doit y avoir un nombre limite.*

The budget wouldn't run to it

I don't think the budget would run to it/stretch to it.

➛ *Je ne pense pas que cela pourrait entrer dans notre budget.*

Written off

Millions of euros have been written off in that venture.

➛ *Des millions d'euros sont passés par pertes et profits dans cette entreprise.*

Round it up

It will be easier if we round it up to the nearest figure.

➛ *Cela sera plus facile si nous arrondissons au chiffre supérieur.*

Work things out to the minimum

If we want to come out even, we'll have to work things out to the minimum.

➛ *Si nous ne voulons pas en être de notre poche, il va falloir calculer au plus juste.*

Scrimp and save

That's what you call cheese paring. And how are we to deliver the goods if we have to scrimp and save?

➛ *C'est ce qu'on appelle des économies de bouts de chandelles. Comment s'imaginent-ils/espèrent-ils que nous allons pouvoir faire face en économisant sur tout ?/Jamais on ne va pouvoir assurer si on doit économiser sur tout.*

III. SUCCESSES SUCCÈS

Take off

His policies have really taken off. They're going with a bang.

➛ *Ses mesures ont le vent en poupe/connaissent un franc succès. Elles vont tambour battant.*

Take a roundabout way into favour

These ideas took a roundabout way into favour.

➛ *Ces idées n'ont trouvé la popularité qu'après bien des détours/ n'ont pas été immédiatement plébiscitées.*

Carry the day

The powers that be are confident that this customer- oriented approach will really carry the day.

➛ *Les grands décideurs sont convaincus qu'une approche orientée vers les clients va remporter/va connaître un franc succès.*

The plan is afoot

The action plan is afoot and coming along.

➛ *Le plan d'action a été mis en œuvre et se concrétise.*

In the straight

Take heart, we're in the straight now/on the final stretch!

➛ *Ce n'est pas le moment de nous décourager, nous sommes dans la dernière ligne droite.*

And then some

They achieved all their objectives and then some.

➛ *Ils ont atteint tous leurs objectifs et les ont même dépassés.*

IV. FAILURES ÉCHECS

Dead in the water

Without us, the project is dead in the water!

➛ *Sans nous, le projet est à l'eau avant même d'avoir vu le jour !*

Head for the rocks

With such strict deadlines, we're heading for the rocks.

➛ *Avec des échéances aussi courtes, nous courons à la catastrophe.*

It never got to first base

A lot of time and effort went into the project but it never got to first base.

➛ *Nous avons beaucoup investi dans ce projet, mais il a tourné court/ n'a jamais vu le jour.*

Fall through

Because of the appalling weather conditions, my entire trip has fallen through/was shot to hell (slang).

➛ *Les conditions météorologiques ayant été exécrables, ma visite a tourné court/a foiré.*

Draw a blank

We were asked to consult the archives on this. But our search drew a blank.

➛ *On nous a demandé de consulter les archives là-dessus, mais nous avons fait chou blanc.*

Pull the plug on

If we don't deliver on the first phase of the project, the chances are that the management will pull the plug on it.

➛ *Si nous n'obtenons pas de résultats dès la phase un du projet, il y a des chances pour que la direction décide de (le) laisser tomber.*

Kick into the long grass

Even though it had potential, the proposal was kicked into the long grass.

➛ *C'est une proposition qui avait de l'avenir, mais elle est passée à la trappe/a été reléguée aux oubliettes.*

He's toast

If the project falls through, he's toast/he's finished. That's what he was appointed for.

➛ *Si le projet échoue, il est grillé. C'était la raison de sa nomination à ce poste.*

Exerting an influence

Influencer autrui

I. INTERACTION INTERAGIR

You had me going there

I had no idea it was a joke. You had me going there!

➛ *Je ne pensais pas que c'était une plaisanterie, j'y ai cru un moment/ j'ai vraiment marché !*

At cross purposes

We are at cross purposes here.

➛ *Nous nous sommes mal compris/il y a quiproquo.*

Nothing gets past you

Nothing gets past you, does it? Not even the smallest print at the bottom of a contract!

➛ *Rien ne vous échappe, n'est-ce pas ? Pas même les clauses en bas de page aussi minuscules soient-elles !*

Throw a wet blanket

His remark threw a wet blanket on the mood of the meeting.

➛ *Ses paroles ont comme jeté un froid pendant la réunion.*

Fraught

The meeting was a bit **fraught**.

➛ *La réunion a été un peu tendue.*

II. MANIPULATION MANIPULER

Sell us a bill of goods

I'm not sure this consulting company isn't trying to sell us a bill of goods/isn't trying to sell us a pup.

➛ *Je me demande si ces consultants n'essaient pas de nous tromper sur la marchandise.*

Sidestep the question

I'm none the wiser on this particular term of the contract, because he kept sidestepping the question.

➛ *Je ne suis pas mieux renseigné/je ne suis pas plus avancé sur cet aspect du contrat, parce qu'il a noyé le poisson/n'a cessé d'éluder la question.*

Dodge

We could sense something was afoot and suspected she was going to quit, but whenever the subject came up, she dodged the questions/ she stonewalled.

➛ *Nous sentions bien qu'il y avait quelque chose, et nous soupçonnions qu'elle allait démissionner, mais elle bottait en touche à chaque fois que le sujet était évoqué.*

Evade the issue

He very skilfully evaded the issue of her departure and made no reference to the game of musical chairs that was going on behind the scenes.

➛ *Il a esquivé la question de son départ et n'a fait aucune référence au jeu de chaises musicales dans les coulisses.*

Hedge

Over the severance packages, she hedged and remained non-committal.

➛ *Sur la question des indemnités de licenciements, elle a manié la langue de bois.*

Fudge the issue

When asked about who was next on the list of boardroom casualties, she fudged the issue by saying that "casualties" was much too strong a word.

➛ *Lorsque nous lui avons demandé qui était la prochaine victime sur la liste des administrateurs, elle a éludé la question/elle a noyé le poisson en disant que « victime » était un terme bien trop fort.*

Smoke and mirrors

Our presentation was far from an exercise in smoke and mirrors. It gave a fair account of the endless and exciting possibilities our new tool will offer.

➛ *Notre présentation était loin d'être de la poudre aux yeux. Elle rendait compte des possibilités infinies qu'ouvre notre nouvel outil.*

Cop out

If we pull out at this stage, they might think we're just copping out.

➛ *Si nous tirons notre épingle du jeu, ils risquent de penser que nous nous défilons.*

A mare's nest

Don't you think that, given the circumstances, a partnership with a start-up will turn out to be just a mare's nest?

➛ *Ne pensez-vous pas que dans ces circonstances, un partenariat avec une petite start-up risque de se révéler très décevant/d'être une chimère/un leurre ?*

Your card is marked

Your card is marked; one more remark like this one and you're out of here!

➛ *Tu es fiché : encore une remarque comme celle-ci et tu prends la porte !*

Wake up to an issue

Headphones will be needed if we are to work in an open plan office. They seem to have only woken up the issue.

➛ *Nous aurons besoin de casques si nous devons travailler en "open space". Ils semblent ne s'en émouvoir/n'en prendre conscience que maintenant.*

Call on

This being so, we can expect further calls on our generosity.

➛ *Cela étant, attendons-nous à ce que l'on fasse encore appel à notre générosité.*

III. INFLUENCING OTHERS AVOIR DE L'IMPACT SUR

Find a response

The things he's saying really find a response in people.

➛ *Ce qu'il dit parle aux gens.*

Strike a chord

What he said about timelines needing to be more realistic struck a chord with me.

➛ *Ce qu'il a dit sur la nécessité d'avoir des échéances plus réalistes m'a parlé.*

Play well with

What he said will not play well with the delegates coming to the Thursday afternoon meeting.

➛ *Ce qu'il a dit ne va pas bien passer auprès des participants à la réunion du jeudi après-midi.*

Impinge on

The decision to redesign the layout of the premises impinges on every aspect of office life.

➛ *La décision de modifier la configuration des lieux affecte/a une incidence sur tous les aspects de la vie au bureau.*

Go down well/badly

His bluntness went down badly.

➛ *Son franc-parler est mal passé/a été mal perçu.*

An axe to grind

I have no particular axe to grind, but I think it would be in the interest of our department to get the subsidies.

➛ *Je ne cherche pas à prêcher pour ma paroisse/je n'ai aucun intérêt personnel à cela, mais c'est à notre service que devraient revenir les subventions.*

Be prevailed upon

He has been prevailed upon to take extraordinary measures to fast-forward the visa request.

➛ *Il s'est laissé persuader de prendre des mesures extraordinaires et d'accélérer l'obtention du visa.*

A kick in the teeth

His summary rejection of my application was a real kick in the teeth.

➛ *Quand il a arbitrairement refusé ma candidature, je me suis pris une sacrée baffe.*

Touch a raw nerve

When I used the word "opportunist", I knew I'd touched a raw nerve.

➛ *Quand j'ai prononcé le mot « opportuniste », j'ai tout de suite compris que j'avais touché la corde sensible.*

IV. PERSUASION PERSUADER

Talk him into

And we'll have to talk him into bringing the date of the seminar forward? That's going to take some doing.

➛ *Et il va falloir le convaincre d'avancer la date du séminaire ? Ce n'est pas gagné d'avance.*

Preach to the converted

I couldn't agree more. You're preaching to the converted, you know/ you're pushing at an open door.

➛ *Je suis évidemment d'accord avec vous. Vous prêchez des convertis.*

On the right side of

We can't afford to antagonise her. Let's stay on the right side of her.

➛ *Nous ne pouvons nous permettre de la contrarier. Essayons de la mettre dans de bonnes dispositions.*

Soft-soap

Come on, I'm not soft-soaping anybody. They just need a bit of persuading, that's all.

➤ *Je ne suis pas en train de leur passer de la pommade. J'exerce juste un peu mon pouvoir persuasif.*

Make all the right noises

At the managers' meeting today, when asked about how I saw the company's prospects for next year, I made all the right noises in their direction.

➤ *À la réunion, quand ils m'ont interrogé(e) sur l'avenir de la société, j'ai dit tout ce qu'il convenait de dire/ce qu'ils étaient disposés à entendre.*

Responding

Réagir

I. ACTING IN HASTE PRÉCIPITATION/RAPIDITÉ

Shoot from the hip

His response was immediate. He shot from the hip.

➛ *Sa réaction ne s'est pas fait attendre. Il a dégainé tout de suite.*

To trump

You trumped me there. I was going to say this later.

➛ *Vous m'avez devancé. Je pensais y venir plus tard.*

Be on the ball

We were swift to deal with their request. That's what you call being on the ball.

➛ *Nous avons été rapides pour traiter leur demande. C'est ce qui s'appelle être au taquet.*

Meet half way

If they aren't trying to meet us half way, then we'll play hardball.

➛ *S'ils ne tentent même pas de faire des compromis, alors on n'aura pas à prendre de gants.*

Play ball

I have my doubts on the implementation of the scheme, but let's play ball and see where it gets us.

➛ *J'ai des doutes sur l'aspect pratique de leur idée, mais jouons le jeu et voyons où cela nous mène.*

Champ at the bit

He was underemployed, over-qualified and champing at the proverbial bit. He kept hoping that things would get going soon.

➛ *Sous-employé, surqualifié, il rongeait son frein comme on dit. Il espérait que les choses allaient se mettre à bouger.*

Pass the buck

When asked about the collapse of the system they passed the buck and said our IT department were responsible.

➛ *Lorsqu'on les a interrogés sur l'échec du système, ils ont fait porter le chapeau à notre service informatique.*

Add fuel to

This merely adds fuel to the guesswork and gossip.

➛ *Ceci ne fait qu'alimenter les conjectures et les commérages.*

A bad-tempered agreement

His haste achieved nothing more than a bad-tempered agreement.

➛ *Sa précipitation n'a conduit à rien d'autre qu'à un accord contraint/dans la mauvaise humeur.*

Go ape

When I said that hiring a consultant for the job wasn't an option, he went ape/flew off the handle/flipped his lid.

➛ *Quand j'ai dit que nous ne pouvions raisonnablement pas embaucher un consultant, il est monté dans les tours.*

Below the parapet

I may be accused of keeping my head below the parapet, but working to a shorter timeframe presents risks that we can't afford to take.

➛ *On m'accusera peut-être de ne pas vouloir me mouiller/d'être frileux mais se fixer des échéances plus courtes comporte des risques que nous ne pouvons nous permettre de prendre.*

Quick off the mark

The whole idea of organising a seminar was a last minute thing; we had to be quick off the mark and make the necessary arrangements forthwith/without delay.

➛ *La décision d'organiser un séminaire ayant été prise à la dernière minute, il nous a fallu être réactifs/dégainer rapidement et nous organiser en conséquence.*

They beat us to it

There was only one videoconference room available, and they beat us to it.

➛ *Il n'y avait qu'une seule salle de vidéoconférence libre, et ils nous ont devancés.*

Jump the gun

The last thing we want is them jumping the gun and sending an invitation to the drinks party when we're not even sure there'll be one.

➛ *La dernière chose que nous voulons c'est qu'ils devancent l'appel/qu'ils agissent prématurément/qu'ils soient trop pressés et envoient une invitation alors qu'aucune confirmation d'un cocktail n'a été apportée.*

Preempt

I preempted him by announcing that I was pulling out of the project.

➛ *J'ai pris les devants en lui annonçant que je me retirais du projet.*

II. FEAR PEUR

Chicken out

They were to send an inflammatory letter of complaint but chickened out.

➛ *Ils avaient décidé d'envoyer un courrier incendiaire, mais ils se sont dégonflés.*

III. ANNOYANCE AGACEMENT

And that's all he can muster?

A 10% rebate on our next order, when he was responsible for ruining our entire freight? And that's all he can muster?

➛ *Un rabais de 10 % sur notre prochaine commande alors que notre entière cargaison a été ruinée par sa faute ? Et c'est tout ce qu'il trouve à dire/Il n'a pas mieux ?*

Alternative time zone

Did they go into some alternative time zone? Were they on another planet?

➛ *Ils n'ont pas tout suivi !/Ils sont à côté de leurs pompes. D'où est-ce qu'ils débarquent ?*

Bang on about

I wish he'd stop banging on about how well his team has performed, I haven't got all day!

➛ *Il ne peut pas arrêter de nous rebattre les oreilles avec ce que son équipe a réussi à faire ? J'ai pas toute la journée, moi/pas que ça à faire !*

A warning shot

If they keep going over our heads to the customers, we'll have to give them a warning shot (over their bows).

➛ *S'ils s'entêtent à s'adresser aux clients sans nous consulter, il faudra lancer un coup de semonce/les rappeler à l'ordre.*

No more dragging it out

Come on. No more dragging it out. The news is that Amanda has given her stamp of approval to our project.

➛ *Allez, venons-en au fait. Amanda a donné son accord au projet.*

IV. EXCESS EXCÈS

Push the envelope

We'll have to ask Kelly to take on the additional task of monitoring progress in Asia as well. That might be pushing the envelope, though.

➛ *Nous devrons demander à Kelly d'ajouter l'Asie à sa charge de travail/ à son périmètre. C'est peut-être trop en demander/ pousser un peu loin/pousser le bouchon trop loin/tirer sur la corde.*

Make an excessive claim on

Hiring a consultant now would be making an excessive claim on our budget.

➛ *L'embauche d'un consultant ponctionnerait notre budget de façon démesurée.*

Work ourselves up into a lather

There's no need to work ourselves up into a lather over his announcement. It will all soon die down.

➛ *Nul besoin de nous mettre dans tous nos états à cause de son annonce. Tout cela va se calmer bientôt.*

All hell to pay

There'll be all hell to pay if the accounts department finds out that your hotel bill is in excess of the company's travel policy.

➛ *Ca va barder si la comptabilité se rend compte que ta note d'hôtel dépasse le budget voyage.*

More than seems warranted

Even if his contribution has been outstanding, offering our HR director's achievements more space in our Newsletter is more than seems warranted.

➛ *La contribution de notre Directeur des Ressources Humaines a été certainement remarquable, mais lui consacrer davantage d'espace dans notre lettre d'information, c'est peut-être en faire un peu trop.*

A "meeting about this meeting"

They're always coming from a "meeting about this meeting".

➛ *Ils ont la réunionite.*

Understatement

She said I'd soon get the hang of it, which has to be the greatest understatement of all time! I know it'll take me years to learn.

➛ *Elle m'a dit que j'apprendrai en deux temps trois mouvements Comme euphémisme on n'a jamais fait mieux ! Il va me falloir des années pour y arriver.*

To cap it all

There was a cluster of people waiting for me and to cap it all, I had to call security to open the conference room for me.

➛ *Les gens étaient à attendre devant la salle de conférence et pour couronner le tout, j'ai dû faire appel à la sécurité pour qu'ils ouvrent la porte.*

That takes the biscuit

Not only do they drown us in paperwork but on top of it, they expect us to return the file by Thursday lunchtime. That takes the biscuit.

➛ *Non seulement ils nous assomment de paperasserie, mais en plus ils veulent le dossier pour jeudi midi ? Ça c'est un comble !*

Dynamics

Dynamique

I. ON THE MOVE MOBILITÉ

Full steam ahead

Now that the team is one member stronger, things are running at full steam ahead.

➛ *L'équipe compte un membre de plus et nous tournons à plein régime maintenant.*

A little further forward

Things sound a little further forward. We're catching up on the backlog.

➛ *On dirait que les choses ont un peu avancé. Nous rattrapons notre retard.*

The prime mover

The prime mover behind this endeavour is our American counterpart.

➛ *L'élément moteur/le principal acteur de cette initiative est notre homologue américain.*

A shot in the arm

Our data cleansing programme hasn't made much progress of late; it needs a shot in the arm.

➛ *Notre programme de nettoyage de données n'a pas beaucoup avancé, il a besoin d'un coup de fouet.*

Rained on his parade

He had great news about the team's latest results, but the announcement of their sister company's closure rained on his parade.

➛ *Il avait une excellente nouvelle quant aux resultats de l'équipe, mais l'annonce de la fermeture de leur société-sœur lui a coupé ses effets/a tout gâché.*

One step forward, two steps back

One step forward, two steps back. We're getting nowhere at all.

➛ *Un pas en avant, deux en arrière. On n'avance pas.*

Back to square one

They seem to have lost the contract so we're back to square one; the whole validation process has to start again.

➛ *Apparemment ils n'ont pas obtenu le contrat, ce qui signifie que le processus de validation est à reprendre : retour à la case départ.*

Boost the energy levels

He made a speech intended to restore confidence among the team and boost the energy levels after such a depleting experience.

➛ *Le but de son discours a été de rétablir la confiance au sein de l'équipe et d'apporter un regain d'énergie, après une expérience aussi démotivante.*

Get cracking

Could you go and get a spare key from Security, we're locked out of the conference room. Get cracking/make it snappy!

➛ *Va chercher un double de la clé au PC Sécurité, nous ne pouvons pas entrer dans la salle de conférence ; il n'y a pas une seconde à perdre !*

It's all systems go

It's all systems go. We'll meet the deadlines.

➛ *Ça turbine un max. On tiendra les délais.*

Shift things up a gear

By forming a partnership with such a prestigious university, our R&D department makes it clear that they are ready to take things up a notch/shift things up a gear and fight off competition.

➛ *À travers son partenariat avec une université prestigieuse comme celle-ci, la R&D montre qu'elle est prête à passer à la vitesse supérieure et à faire face à la concurrence.*

Hobbled by

The company is hobbled by the Research and Development costs.

➛ *La société peine sous le poids des coûts induits par la R&D.*

Hamstrung by

We were to develop links with a university abroad, only to find that we are hamstrung by complex procedures and regulations.

➛ *L'idée était de tisser des liens avec une université à l'étranger, mais nous nous retrouvons paralysés par la complexité des règlements et procédures.*

Short of stalling

The survey results are unlikely to come in any time soon, the research our consultants are conducting is just short of stalling.

➛ *Les résultats de l'enquête ne sont pas prêts d'arriver, la recherche menée par nos consultants est pratiquement au point mort.*

It's all over bar the shouting

The CEO has okayed our project. It's only a matter of days before it is officially signed. I'm pleased to say it's all over bar the shouting.

➛ *Le directeur général a donné le feu vert à notre projet et le signera d'ici quelques jours. J'ai le plaisir de vous dire que c'est gagné/l'important est fait, il ne reste plus que les détails.*

Flatline

The results have more or less flatlined.

➛ *Les résultats ont plus ou moins stagné.*

Fall short

Your end of year review is the ideal time to see where you excel and where you fall short.

➛ *Votre entretien de fin d'année est l'occasion de faire le point sur là où vous êtes performants et là où vous ne l'êtes pas.*

Lose ground

Now would be the time to put our heads together and determine what we are getting right and where we're losing ground.

➛ *Le moment parait opportun de nous concerter et de déterminer là où notre approche est bonne et là où nous perdons du terrain.*

We've seen the worst of the crisis

The figures say that we've seen the worst of the crisis.

➛ *Les chiffres disent que le pire de la crise est derrière nous.*

We aren't making a lot of ground

We've approached the top management for a possible involvement of our sister company in the current project, but we aren't making a lot of ground.

➛ *Nous avons soumis à la direction l'idée d'une éventuelle collaboration de notre société-sœur à l'actuel projet, mais nous n'avançons guère.*

II. COMPETITION CONCURRENCE

Hot on their heels

With the competition hot on their heels, they can feel the pressure is mounting.

➛ *Avec la concurrence qui les talonne, la pression monte.*

Steal a march on

Our competitors tried to steal a march on us by offering more favourable contract terms to Tazina & co. But our reputation stood us in good stead.

➛ *Ils ont tenté de nous damer le pion et proposé des termes de contrat plus intéressants à la société Tazina & co. Mais notre réputation nous a été d'un grand secours.*

Limp on

We wonder how long the business will limp on, and we're doing our best to keep it ticking over.

➛ *Allons savoir combien de temps l'affaire va se maintenir ! Nous faisons de notre mieux pour qu'elle continue de tourner bon an, mal an.*

Beat them to the draw

We'll have to beat them to the draw and apply first.

➛ *Il nous faudra dégainer plus vite et nous inscrire en premier.*

Be one down on

We didn't want to be one down on them, so we set up our own intranet site.

➛ *Nous ne voulions pas être en reste et avons donc mis en place notre propre site intranet.*

III. COHESION COHÉSION

Hard wired into

Change management is hard wired into our project.

➛ *L'accompagnement au changement est ancré dans notre projet.*

The bigger picture

Introducing the consultants to the team was a good move. Now we are aware of how their tasks fit into the bigger picture.

➛ *L'initiative de présenter les consultants à l'équipe était excellente. Nous savons enfin comment leur mission s'inscrit dans le cadre général.*

Of a piece with

The current freeze on new staff appointments is wholly of a piece with the company's cost reduction effort.

➛ *L'actuel gel des embauches s'inscrit dans le prolongement de la politique de réduction des coûts de l'entreprise.*

Competing imperatives

There's no easy way out of this as we are confronting two competing imperatives.

➛ *Il n'y a pas de solution simple, nous sommes face à deux impératifs inconciliables.*

Hang together

Given time you will understand how the whole R&D department hangs together and who does what.

➛ *Avec un peu de temps, tu comprendras comment le département de R&D s'articule et qui fait quoi.*

The keystone

Our project is the keystone of our company's HR model.

➛ *Notre projet est la clé de voûte de notre modèle RH.*

Communication

Communication

I. PUBLIC RELATIONS RELATIONS AVEC LE PUBLIC

Pitched at the right level

The introductory speech must be pitched at the right level.

➛ *Le discours d'introduction doit être adapté à l'auditoire.*

Stay on message

We need to stay on message.

➛ *Il nous faut rester cohérents par rapport au message que nous voulons faire passer.*

Hard to shift

The perception is hard to shift.

➛ *C'est une image bien ancrée dans les têtes/Les gens restent avec cette idée.*

Enlist the help of

Our on-site disability awareness week was successful. We'd enlisted the help of local groups and charities.

➛ *Notre semaine de sensibilisation aux handicaps a été un succès. Nous avions recueilli le soutien d'associations locales.*

All hype and little substance

It's all hype and little substance.

➛ *C'est beaucoup de grands mots et peu de contenu.*

Resonate with

What he said will resonate with many/will strike a chord with many/will ring a bell with many.

➛ *Beaucoup se retrouveront dans ce qu'il a dit/ce qu'il a dit trouvera un écho chez beaucoup*

Starved of information

We were drowning in data but starved of information.

➛ *L'abondance de données ne rassasiait pas notre faim d'informations.*

An emotive issue

Animal experimentation can be an emotive issue and the pharmaceutical industry has to face up to it.

➛ *Il arrive que l'expérimentation sur les animaux déchaîne les passions, c'est une chose que l'industrie pharmaceutique doit assumer.*

A makeover

Our intranet home page has yet to have a serious makeover.

➛ *La page d'accueil de notre intranet a besoin d'une sérieuse cure de jouvence/d'un sérieux « lifting ».*

Strike home

What he said about timelines needing to be more realistic struck home to me.

➛ *Ce qu'il a dit sur la nécessité d'avoir des échéances plus réalistes m'a parlé.*

The signal we want to send

The signal we want to send is that both our teams work together towards the same goal.

➛ *Le message que nous voulons faire passer est que nos deux équipes sont solidaires et travaillent dans un but commun.*

Create hype

Creating hype certainly gets people interested, but is it desirable when it comes to introducing our new manager?

➛ *Créer un effet d'annonce suscite l'intérêt des gens, mais est-ce souhaitable quand il s'agit de l'arrivée de notre nouveau directeur ?*

Catch the mood of

His speech caught the mood of the assembly.

➛ *Son discours était en phase avec son auditoire.*

Defuse a crisis

We'll have to defuse a potentially severe crisis and reassure users that the computer failure will soon be put right.

➣ *Il va falloir désamorcer une crise potentiellement grave en rassurant les utilisateurs sur le fait que la panne informatique sera vite réparée.*

Showcasing

They forgot that the event wasn't about showcasing, but actually about building trust with our prospective customers.

➣ *Ils ont oublié que l'objectif du salon n'était pas de présenter une belle vitrine/de faire une opération de prestige, mais de construire des relations de confiance avec des clients.*

II. PUBLIC SPEAKING DISCOURS

Cut to the chase

I'll cut to the chase, and break the news we've all be waiting for.

➣ *Je vais aller droit à l'essentiel. Voici la nouvelle que nous attendions tous.*

A smooth transition

Your last remark provides an appropriate and smooth transition to the topic I'd like to address.

➣ *Cette remarque m'amène naturellement à la question que je voulais aborder.*

End of aside

End of aside. I don't want to bore you with the details.

➣ *Fin de parenthèse. Je ne voudrais pas vous ennuyer en donnant trop de détails.*

Which is saying something

Mercek has agreed to work in partnership with us, – which is saying something because we know them to be very choosy.

➣ *Mercek a accepté de devenir notre partenaire, et ce n'est pas peu dire, puisque nous savons qu'ils sont très sélectifs.*

Back to where we came in

This takes us back to where we came in.

➣ *Cela nous ramène à ce que nous disions au début de notre discussion.*

A good lead-in

A good lead-in to what I'd like to talk about.

➣ *Ceci est une bonne entrée en matière/une bonne introduction aux questions que je devais aborder.*

The operative word

"Caution" being the operative word here.

➣ *Le mot « prudence » étant le mot clé dans ce cas particulier.*

Sit well in context

The word "lengthy" in "lengthy negotiations" doesn't sit well in context. It gives the idea that they were drawn-out and tedious, which they weren't!

➣ *Le terme « longues » dans « longues négociations » ne convient pas dans ce contexte. On en conclut qu'elles ont été fastidieuses et sans fin, ce qui n'est pas le cas.*

Dwell on

I don't mean to dwell on the negative.

➣ *Mon intention n'est pas de m'attarder sur le négatif.*

Interject

If I could just interject for a moment: "can you put a price tag on the scheme?"

➣ *Je voudrais faire une petite parenthèse : ce plan a-t-il été chiffré ?*

III. CONFIDENTIALITY CONFIDENTIALITÉ

Best not committed to paper

What we've been saying here is best not committed to paper.

➣ *Il est préférable de ne pas consigner ce qui vient d'être dit.*

IV. CLARIFICATION CLARIFICATION

Shed some light on

We'll ask our local Scrooge to shed some light on those figures.

➛ *Nous allons demander à notre Harpagon/notre grigou de comptable de nous éclairer sur ces chiffres.*

V. INFORMATION INFORMATION

Be wise to the fact

I hope they are wise to the fact that they aren't going to be paid extra hours.

➛ *J'espère qu'ils sont bien conscients du fait qu'ils ne seront pas payés en heures supplémentaires/qu'ils en ont été informés.*

In some detail

The attached document lays out the plan in some detail.

➛ *Vous trouverez le plan exposé de façon assez détaillée dans la pièce jointe.*

VI. BEING UNBIASED IMPARTIALITÉ

Give an equal hearing to

We need to give an equal hearing to both approaches.

➛ *Il nous faut accorder une oreille attentive et impartiale aux deux points de vue.*

Miscellaneous

Divers

I. BUILDING ON/SETTING THE FOUNDATIONS
ÉLABORATION/MÉTHODE

Rough out

I've roughed out some ideas.

➛ *J'ai ébauché quelques idées.*

Float an idea

She floated the idea of issuing a monthly newsletter.

➛ *Elle a émis l'idée d'une publication mensuelle.*

Bounce a few ideas off someone

Maybe if we are creative enough, we'll find a way round the problem. I'll bounce a few ideas off our Change Manager.

➛ *Peut-être en étant plus inventifs pourrons-nous contourner le problème ? Je vais soumettre mes quelques idées à notre Directeur de la communication et voir ce qu'il en pense/je vais tester mes idées avec notre directeur.*

On the drawing board

That's not all, there's more on the drawing board.

➛ *Cela ne s'arrête pas là, il y en a encore à l'étude.*

In the melting pot

We are more than happy to welcome him on board, but he hasn't yet made his decision. It's all in the melting pot.

➛ *Nous sommes très heureux de l'accueillir au sein de notre équipe, mais il n'a pas encore pris sa décision. Les choses en sont au stade des discussions.*

Back in the melting pot

Following the sudden departure of the production manager, the whole thing is back in the melting pot.

➛ *Après le départ précipité du directeur de production tout est remis en question.*

Bat the idea around

I'm quite in favour of it. Now that we are all seated around the table, I suggest we bat the idea around to see what you think of it.

➛ *L'idée me plaît bien. Puisque nous sommes tous réunis, mettons la sur la table et discutons-en/et voyons ce qu'elle donne.*

Come away from a meeting

I came away from the meeting brimming with ideas on what my intranet homepage layout could be.

➛ *En sortant de la réunion, j'étais plein(e) d'idées sur la façon dont ma page d'accueil sur l'intranet se présenterait.*

Take away

There is one thing in particular I took away from this meeting.

➛ *J'ai retenu/retiré une chose de cette réunion.*

Worth airing

Your idea is worth airing. It will be interesting to test the water and see what people think.

➛ *Cela vaudra la peine de mettre votre question sur le tapis. Ce sera intéressant de tâter le terrain et de la soumettre à un examen collectif.*

A half-way house for

This solution offers a half-way house for both those in favour of the project and those against.

➛ *C'est une solution intermédiaire/solution qui offre un compromis aux détracteurs comme aux défenseurs du projet.*

Makeshift

Cindy will be sharing her office with Ram, but this can only be a makeshift arrangement. They both need their space.

➛ *Cindy partagera son bureau avec Ram, mais ceci est une solution de pis-aller. Tous les deux ont besoin de leur espace de travail.*

II. ACHIEVEMENTS AND KNOW-HOW PROUESSE/SAVOIR-FAIRE

A balancing act

Going all out on our project and staying on budget will be a difficult balancing act.

➛ *Entre respecter notre budget et investir à fond dans notre projet, le grand écart va être rude.*

A high wire act

Negotiating with the trade-unions over pre-retirement plans is going to be a high wire act for the management.

➛ *La négociation des plans de préretraite avec les syndicats promet d'être un numéro de corde raide.*

A juggling act

I've got to speak at the conference on Tuesday morning and my report is due in on the same day, so I'm going to have to do a bit of a juggling act.

➛ *J'interviens à la conférence de mardi matin et dois rendre mon rapport le même jour : je vais devoir jongler.*

You drove the project through

You drove the project through. You deserve to get the credit.

➛ *C'est vous qui avez mené le projet à son terme. C'est à vous que revient le mérite.*

III. OUR PLACE ON THE SCENE OF WORLD AFFAIRS
POSITIONNEMENT SUR L'ÉCHIQUIER MONDIAL

In the driving seat

On the Asian market, our Singapore-based branch is in the driving seat.

➣ *Notre succursale de Singapour est leader/est bien établie sur le marché asiatique/tient le haut du pavé.*

A foothold

If we want to gain a foothold in the market, we need to offer innovative products and carry out a thorough market research.

➣ *Si nous voulons commencer à pénétrer le marché, nous devons présenter des produits innovants et faire une étude de marché poussée.*

Hog the limelight

They tend to hog the limelight, but surely we can't freeze them out.

➣ *Ils ont tendance à occuper le terrain ; on ne peut pas pour autant les tenir à l'écart.*

IV. INDIVIDUALS AUTRUI

Tread carefully

In matters of seating arrangements, we need to tread carefully. The last thing we want is a diplomatic incident.

➣ *S'agissant du plan de table, nous allons essayer de ménager les susceptibilités. Nous n'avons pas besoin d'un incident diplomatique.*

Tiptoe around

I'm afraid the pressure he's under isn't helping at the moment; we have to keep tiptoeing carefully around him.

➣ *La pression actuelle n'arrange rien, il faut le ménager/y aller doucement avec lui en ce moment.*

Get on the wrong side of

We have our hands tied. We don't want to get on the wrong side of the management, and yet we can't make progress without the risk of displeasing them.

➢ *Nous avons les mains liées, il n'est pas question de nous faire mal voir par la direction et pourtant nous ne pouvons avancer sans risquer de les froisser.*

Not a details man

He's not a details man. The up side is that it helps him make difficult decisions sometimes.

➢ *Il n'est pas du genre à s'encombrer de détails. L'avantage est qu'il sait trancher quand cela s'impose.*

Sit uncomfortably with

Her position of authority sits uncomfortably with her rebellious streak.

➢ *Son poste de responsabilité ne cadre pas avec son côté rebelle.*

A wolf in sheep's clothing

A wolf in sheep's clothing.

➢ *Un loup déguisé en agneau.*

V. TAKE YOUR PICK FAITES VOTRE CHOIX

Blow the deadlines

Blow the deadlines! If it takes another two weeks to reach an agreement, we won't settle for one.

➢ *Tant pis pour les échéances ! Si c'est deux semaines qu'il nous faut, on n'en prendra pas qu'une seule !*

Big cheese

He/she's big cheese/a big wig/head Honcho.

➢ *C'est un gros bonnet.*

Put the issue to bed

Could we put the issue to bed? Time is running out.

➛ *Pourrions-nous clore le sujet ? Nous n'avons plus beaucoup de temps.*

By the bucket load

He was in Shanghai for only a few days, but gathered bucket loads of information. I can't wait to read his paper information.

➛ *Il n'a passé que tois jours à Shanghai, mais a réuni des informations à la pelle. Je suis vraiment curieux de lire son rapport.*

The latest instalment in

The latest instalment in the lingering/ongoing feud between the three departments.

➛ *Le tout dernier épisode du roman feuilleton des querelles entre les trois services.*

Fall in well with

The decision fell in very well with our plans.

➛ *La décision était parfaitement en accord avec nos plans.*

... PART FOUR ...

Keep your hair on
Restons calmes

INTRODUCTION

To someone not involved in the business world, the day to day situations in which assistants can find themselves are a mixture of the incongruous, the absurd, and sometimes even the comical: heart-stopping moments when a conference pin number fails to open a TC, or their counterpart across the Atlantic appears voiceless on the screen as they start their carefully rehearsed videoconference. Times when bureaucracy goes mad and causes new pressures and unending chains of e-mails; when the computer crashes; when printers become temperamental, and phone calls that keep leading to voice mails never reach the person for whom they are intended.

Drawing on memories from my own personal experience I remember once putting things in place for what was intended to be "the perfect visit" for our choice American guests. I had scheduled a tightly-knit programme, ordered the taxis, included staggered collections from reception in the order in which each visitor arrived; back to back meetings with the various managers; a customised meal at the Company Club with waiter to boot, and had planned it to end just in time for taxi rides back to the airport so that our guests could quickly hop onto another plane. However, this was counting without accommodating very last minute changes due to diary constraints: my best laid plans had suddenly gone awry; the stylish meal whose preparation had involved me in hours of conversation with the Chef had to be consumed in unseemly haste to the accompaniment of the ominously ticking clock.

On another occasion, I was asked in all haste late one Friday evening to free up a particular room (S11 as I seem to recall) for the following week five days running. This was on account of top priority tests which were to be conducted urgently. S11 had been claimed by a number of occupants already and I sweated blood to make contact with each single one of them. They were not picking up, which meant I had to climb up one flight of stairs and walk into meetings to get whoever was concerned to cancel their reservations. Prior to this I had worked out an alternative room for each, and had actually booked it to ensure that no time was wasted. In one and a half hours I had managed to wrap the whole thing up, only to find on the following Monday morning, that room S11 was empty and not needed after all. This was more than enough to compromise whatever benefits the weekend had provided.

The assistant's time and energy are sometimes wasted on an anxious manager's whim or hasty decisions. If on occasion I could be time-travelled into the past, I would completely rewrite some of the scenarios and opt for being kinder to myself and go for solutions less trying on the nerves. Experience matters. Experience will prompt you to say: "Let's set out a few ground rules. How urgent is this?", or "This is something massive you're asking, what kind of deadline did you have in mind?"

Polite and not so polite pointers

Dire avec ou sans gants

When you feel...	Polite and not so polite pointers
...your efforts are not being rewarded ➛ *Que vos efforts ne sont pas reconnus*	▪ "Surely this deserves some appreciation; I went above and beyond to make this get-together happen." ▪ "A thank you wouldn't go amiss."
...overwhelmed with work ➛ *Que vous n'en pouvez plus*	▪ "It's time you started delegating a little more to the other members of the team." ▪ "Somebody's landed a problem on me, hasn't he/hasn't she?" ▪ "It looks like I've inherited the in-box from hell; let's take one step at a time, shall we?" ▪ (Rising to the challenge)"God loves a trier" ▪ "I'm being chief cook and bottle washer, here." ▪ "I've got a lot on my plate at the moment. Never mind, tomorrow is another day." ▪ "I feel as if I'm holding down two jobs." ▪ "Never mind one job; it feels like I've got two." ▪ "Time for me to shut down and forget about my day at work!" ▪ "I don't want to die in harness!"
...you are dealing with obnoxious characters ➛ *Que vous avez à faire avec des personnages odieux*	▪ (Taking a deep breath) "Your request will be top priority as soon as I can see light at the end of the tunnel." ▪ "Are you expecting me to dance attendance on everyone?"

··➤

...you are dealing with obnoxious characters ➛ *Que vous avez à faire avec des personnages odieux*	▪ "I'm not your personal servant!" ▪ "What did your last servant die of?" ▪ "You've got one hell of a complaint coming your way!" ▪ "Someone will be in the dog house if he/she's not careful." ▪ "I'll have your scalp for a duster." ▪ "I'll have your guts for garters." ▪ "I feel like biting somebody's head off." ▪ "I'm not going to dignify that with an answer!" ▪ "I don't want him to take whatever's bugging him out on me!"
...you're having a time of it ➛ *Que vous serrez les dents*	▪ "I've had more than my fair share to do since I came in this morning." ▪ "I need a caffeine boost this morning/my coffee fix." ▪ "My nerves are shot to pieces. I need to pull myself together" ▪ "I need to take a deep breath and get a grip." ▪ "At this time of the day how can I muster up the energy to get this done? It's time to call it a day." ▪ "The state she has whipped me up into with all her hyper preparations!"
...your colleague keeps complaining ➛ *Que vos collègues ne cessent de geindre*	▪ "I'll take care of it, seeing as you're asking with such grace and charm." ▪ "She /He is a 'glass half empty' kind of person, always so negative."

···➤

...you are up against disorganised people ➛ *Qu'il faut vous coltiner des collègues mal organisés*	▪ "If all goes according to plan, we might achieve some miraculous measure of order." ▪ "Dealing with this lot is like herding cats!" ▪ "Today would be good!" ▪ "He's really doing my head in, if only he could be more focused." ▪ "What's all that faffing around in aid of?"

Office life

La vie au bureau

I. ON THE OFFICE PREMISES AU BUREAU

The documents have only just come in from the other site via the internal post.

➛ *Nous venons de recevoir les documents de notre autre site par courrier interne.*

He popped by five minutes ago/stopped by five minutes ago, you've just missed him!

➛ *Il est passé il y a cinq minutes*

If you clap eyes on him let me know straight away.

➛ *Si tu l'aperçois/si tu arrives à le voir, préviens-moi tout de suite.*

You need to collar him as soon as he walks in the door.

➛ *Mettez lui la main dessus/coincez-le dès qu'il passe la porte.*

I'm sorry to hear you're not feeling too good. ***I'll look in on you*** later to see how you're doing.

➛ *Je passerai voir comment ça va*

You go on to the meeting; ***I'll be right behind you***.

➛ *je te rejoins tout de suite.*

I'll be right over/***I'll be along*** to talk to you shortly.

➛ *J'arrive dans une minute.*

Are those the office supplies? If so, ***you'll need showing where to put them***.

➛ *je vais vous montrer où les poser.*

Is it all right if we pop up to see you now? We'll take the stairs; the lift is a bit dodgy today.

➛ *Ça va si je monte te voir maintenant ?*

I'm literally going out of the door as we speak; I'll see you at the cafeteria. Save me a seat.
➣ *Je sors à l'instant*

I was almost out of the door, when you called.
➣ *J'allais pour sortir quand tu m'as appelée.*

We seem to keep missing, don't we?
➣ *On dirait qu'on n'arrive jamais à se voir/qu'on est toujours entre deux.*

Thomas asked me to ***drop in his travel expense sheet*** for him.
➣ *déposer sa note de frais*

II. REMOVALS DÉMÉNAGEMENTS

This is ***our third round trip*** and we need all hands on deck.
➣ *notre troisième aller-retour*

She's on her way over from our new site.
➣ *Elle arrive de notre nouveau site/elle est en chemin.*

Even though I've been here a week, ***I'm still finding my feet***.
➣ *je cherche encore un peu mes marques.*

The telephone engineers ***are*** currently ***putting in new phone lines***.
➣ *installent des lignes téléphoniques supplémentaires.*

It's mayhem, here. There isn't a spare surface anywhere.
➣ *C'est un vrai capharnaüm.*

I turned out the cupboards but I can't find the cable you need.
➣ *J'ai entièrement vidé les placards*

I'll take the parcel to the mail room and tell them that it needs to *be* ***bubble-wrapped*** to avoid damage.
➣ *être dans du papier bulle*

III. TIME SPENT DURING THE OFFICE DAY/WORKING HOURS
LES HORAIRES

It's high time you pushed off, haven't you got a home to go to?
➛ *Tu devrais être partie/il est grand temps que tu t'en ailles*

In the majority of cases my colleague ***doesn't clock off*** before 6 pm. She's here forever!
➛ *ne quitte pas le bureau/ne sort jamais avant*

I don't usually clock on before 9.30 am.
➛ *Je n'arrive pas avant*

It's not going to happen; ***I can't get off early*** today.
➛ *je ne peux pas me libérer tôt*

We need to break off and have a coffee.
➛ *Il faut que nous fassions une pause*

It's time to shut up shop and go home.
➛ *Il est temps de fermer la boutique*

Okay, ***let's call it a day***.
➛ *ça suffira pour aujourd'hui.*

It's time I turned in.
➛ *Il est temps que je me rentre.*

Work follows you home.
➛ *Vous ne décrochez jamais vraiment du boulot même une fois de retour à la maison.*

IV. BUSY TIMETABLES — EMPLOIS DU TEMPS DE MINISTRE

If I don't dedicate some time to my in-basket today, I'll ***end up with an unmanageable backlog***.
➛ *me retrouver avec une pile de choses à rattraper/ça va être impossible de gérer mon retard.*

I'll soon have my head above water; I've been wading through an ocean of e-mails all morning.

➣ *J'y verrai bientôt plus clair ; j'ai passé ma matinée à éplucher mes mails.*

Life is getting back to a more manageable routine, after last week's spate of work.

➣ *Les choses se stabilisent un peu après le surcroît de travail la semaine dernière/une semaine charrette.*

I can freewheel a little, now that most of the team are on holiday, and get down to doing the things I've been putting off.

➣ *Je peux lever le pied un peu*

I'm being press-ganged into a lot of work connected with that file.

➣ *J'ai vraiment la pression et il y a un nombre infini de choses à faire en lien avec ce dossier.*

I have so many priorities; I'm starting to ***fall behind***.

➣ *prendre du retard.*

Having been on holiday, ***I'm left with a slew of messages***.

➣ *mon répondeur est saturé/je me retrouve avec un nombre incalculable de messages/un monceau de messages.*

Your text got to me just as I was about to start the conference call.

➣ *J'ai reçu votre texto au moment même où j'allais commencer la téléconference.*

I hardly have time to draw breath, I'm inundated with work.

➣ *J'ai à peine le temps de reprendre mon souffle*

With ***all the work I've committed myself to*** this month; I've had no time to make headway with that file.

➣ *tout le travail auquel je me suis consacré*

I'm a bit up against it, actually, so I'll have to put this on the back burner for the time being.

➣ *Ca ne va pas être facile/je suis un peu charrette ; pour l'instant, je ne vais pas en faire une priorité.*

The meeting minutes hang over you if you don't deal with them promptly.

➛ *Tant que les minutes ne sont pas faites, ça te prend la tête/tu n'en sors pas.*

It's building up at the moment, it will probably be full on by the middle of the week.

➛ *Pour l'instant les choses se mettent en route ; c'est sans doute en milieu de semaine prochaine que ça va être intensif.*

In preparation for a busy day.

I have done twice my usual stint this week; we urgently need to find a temporary replacement for Elaine.

➛ *J'ai fait le double de travail*

I had to go through all the admin stuff, which took an age.

➛ *J'ai dû me coltiner toute la paperasserie, et ça m'a pris un temps monstrueux.*

I've been working myself to the bone.

➛ *J'ai travaillé d'arrache-pied.*

They worked until their eyes dropped out yesterday.

➛ *Ils avaient les yeux qui se croisaient hier tellement ils avaient travaillé.*

There are ***things running me late***.

➛ *choses qui me retardent/me mettent en retard.*

My time gets eaten into by people who keep interrupting me and sidetracking me.

➛ *Je suis sans cesse interrompu(e) , ça me disperse et ça mange mon temps.*

I've really kicked off a lot of things; I need to see them through.

➛ *J'ai lancé beaucoup de choses, il me faut les mener à bien.*

V. GETTING STARTED À VOS MARQUES !

I've got my brain in gear now, fire away!/I'm all ears.
➛ *Ça y est je suis prêt. J'y vois plus clair maintenant, allez-y, j'écoute !*

I'm getting myself together; I'll be ready in five minutes.
➛ *Je me prépare*

I need to pull myself together after such a trying day yesterday.
➛ *Il faut que je me remette de la journée épuisante d'hier.*

Are you ***all fired up*** and ready to go?
➛ *prêt à bondir ?*

Just shaping up for my medical visit.
➛ *Je me prépare psychologiquement pour*

You're ready for the off? Let's go to lunch!
➛ *Tu es sur le départ/prêt à démarrer ?*

I'm in the middle of getting my act together for my 9 am appointment with my boss.
➛ *Je suis en train de m'organiser pour*

VI. ORGANISATIONAL SKILLS SAVOIR S'ORGANISER

Start ticking tasks off. That will give you a clearer picture of what remains to be done.
➛ *Commencez à cocher les choses au fur et à mesure qu'elles sont faites.*

I hoped things would be further on.
➛ *J'espérais que les choses auraient avancé/que nous en serions plus loin.*

Once you've got your list into shape, you'll be half way there.
➛ *Une fois que tu auras dressé une liste, tu auras fait la moitié du chemin.*

Let me see which items will have to slip down on the priority list.
➛ *Montre-moi dans ta liste ce qui ne devra plus être classé comme prioritaire.*

You've got to get eveything done when it needs doing.

→ *Il faut faire les choses en temps voulu/il ne faut pas laisser traîner les choses.*

I've done that, so, ***one less thing to think about***!

→ *Ça sera toujours ça de moins à penser !*

I did various outstanding tasks; however, I still have a couple more things to finish.

→ *J'ai réglé pas mal de choses en suspens*

I'm already getting my head round the forthcoming seminar.

→ *J'ai déjà commencé à réfléchir au prochain séminaire.*

VII. JOB DESCRIPTION/ACTIVITY
UNE JOURNÉE AU TRAVAIL

The next two days will be spent ***initiating my successor***/ replacement.

→ *à former la personne qui me remplace.*

We are ***bombarded with bumf*** relentlessly

→ *assaillis de paperasse*

She's finding it hard to ***engage with office life; it's her first assignment***.

→ *se mettre à la vie de bureau ; c'est sa première mission.*

Can you ***try tracking down*** the contract in your files?

→ *essayer de trouver, mettre la main sur*

I've been rooting around all morning and still can't find the keys to the filing cabinet.

→ *J'ai cherché, fouillé partout*

It would be a good idea to prepare a detailed list of ***discrepancies*** and reasons for variances between the budget and the forecast.

→ *écarts entre*

I'll write up the minutes while things are hot on the anvil/fresh in my mind/on top of my head. ***If not I'll be struggling later.***

➛ *Je vais me mettre aux comptes-rendus dans la foulée/et battre le fer tant qu'il est chaud. Sinon après je vais ramer.*

It was left to me to assign a reviewer to each abstract sent.

➛ *C'est à moi qu'il est incombé/qu'il est revenu d'affecter un relecteur à chacun des abrégés que nous recevons.*

I chased them up for those files this morning. It can take anything up to 5 days.

➛ *Je les ai relancés pour ces dossiers*

I have addressed all your outstanding issues, what would you like me to start on next?

➛ *J'ai traité tous les dossiers en suspens*

VIII. HARDWARE/EQUIPMENT RESTER CONNECTÉ

The proposal's just printing out now.

➛ *Elle/il est en train d'imprimer la proposition.*

I am still processing.

➛ *Mon ordinateur rame.*

Just let me connect my computer to the ***docking station***.

➛ *station d'accueil.*

Whilst it's booting up, let's discuss the files we want to share.

➛ *Pendant qu'il démarre*

Before the computer fires up this morning, I'll have the time to get a coffee and make a few phone calls.

➛ *Avant que mon ordinateur se mette en route*

You hook up your computer to the screen and the slides are projected on to it.

➛ *Tu relies ton ordinateur à l'écran*

Log off your computer and switch it off at the mains as you leave your office.
➣ *Déconnectez-vous et débranchez l'ordinateur*

It's important to ***shut down a programme*** correctly.
➣ *fermer un programme*

I can't believe we're lumbered with that old gas-powered computer!
➣ *Je ne comprends pas qu'on puisse nous refiler un ordinateur qui date de Mathusalem/un vieux clou comme ça !*

IX. BACK TO PAPER À LA PLUME ET AU CRAYON

I have got it ***in long hand*** on 4 sides of A4.
➣ *écrit à la main*

It's covered with crossings-out; I need a clean draft for tomorrow.
➣ *C'est plein de ratures*

Let me just grab a pen, I'll jot it down.
➣ *Attends, je prends un stylo. Je note ça.*

My pen seems to have walked.
➣ *Mon stylo s'est volatilisé.*

Sometimes I tear open envelopes, only to realise they were not intended for me!
➣ *Parfois j'ouvre l'enveloppe d'un coup et je m'aperçois qu'elle ne m'était pas adressée.*

When doing the mailing, be sure to seal the envelopes correctly, ***otherwise the business card might fall out***.
➣ *sinon la carte de visite risque de glisser.*

They don't accept paper copies, so ***I'll e-mail it over to them***.
➣ *je leur ferai parvenir par mail.*

X. WORD PROCESSING | TRAITEMENT DE TEXTE

I thought I was typing in caps, when suddenly I realised I was ***in lower case***.

➛ *en minuscules*

This is the format of the word document ***as it came through to me***.

➛ *comme il m'est arrivé/tel que je l'ai reçu.*

On the document I have e-mailed, are you able to ***locate the references*** I've given you?

➛ *repérer les références*

The material ***is sourced from*** SAP.

➛ *provient de*

The decimal point has moved by 2 places.

➛ *La virgule a été décalée de deux chiffres.*

I've touch-typed my e-mail; you may find a couple of typos.

➛ *J'ai tapé mon mail sans regarder le clavier ; il peut y avoir des coquilles.*

I discovered ***that the entire text came out in upper case***. That treacherous Caps Lock key!

➛ *que tout le texte était tapé en majuscules*

Can you ***take out one space*** between those two words?

➛ *supprimer l'espace en trop entre les deux mots ?*

He's the second one down on the list.

➛ *Il est en deuxième position sur la liste.*

I'm calling the document up on my screen.

➛ *J'ouvre le document à l'écran.*

You'll have to scroll down in the body of the e-mail to find what you're looking for.

➛ *L'information que tu cherches est dans le corps du mail, continue à descendre.*

To de-clutter my e-mail box, I'll have to get rid of all attachments.
➛ *Pour alléger ma boîte/ma boîte de réception*

The paging is out; we need to re-number the pages.
➛ *Il y a un décalage dans la pagination/le numéro des pages est décalé.*

Haven't you spotted the misprint ***five lines from the end of the text***/ from the bottom of the page?
➛ *cinq lignes avant la fin du texte ?*

You need to convert your documents to PDF format.

... PART FIVE ...

Write your own
À vous maintenant !

THE SECRET OF SUCCESS IS PREPARATION

I - CLERICAL FUNCTIONS

a map giving travel directions	CLERICAL/Restaurants/Invitation to business breakfasts
a juggle fitting everything in	CLERICAL/Difficulties in setting up an appointment/Busy schedules
turnout	CLERICAL/Restaurants/Preparation
found a suitable place	CLERICAL/Restaurants/Choosing a venue
nursing her drink	CLERICAL/Restaurants/ At the restaurant
sent out the invitations	CLERICAL/Restaurants/Preparation
the team's accomplishments	CLERICAL/Restaurants/Preparation
colour scheme keyed to	CLERICAL/Organising a seminar/ Organising/Colour scheme, freebies
in recognition of everybody's hard work,	CLERICAL/Restaurants/Invitation to business breakfasts
you can never be overdressed for this kind of event	CLERICAL/Restaurants/ At the restaurant

...➤

II - TALKING THE TALK

good feedback from our guests	TALKING THE TALK/Being positive/ Appreciation of Hard work
no mean feat	TALKING THE TALK/Being positive/ Appreciation of Hard work
all part of the service	TALKING THE TALK/Facilitators/ The ready word

III - A PHRASE A DAY

a whole set of circumstances	A PHRASE A DAY/Insight/ Analysis-point of view
it wouldn't look good	A PHRASE A DAY/Insight/ Analysis-point of view
a moot point	A PHRASE A DAY/Insight/ Arguing the case
would the team sustain the pace	A PHRASE A DAY/Staying power/ Pressure
a few removes from	A PHRASE A DAY/Insight/ Clearsightedness

IV - KEEP YOUR HAIR ON

all the work he had committed himself to	KEEP YOUR HAIR ON/Office life/ Busy timetables
had been working himself to the bone	KEEP YOUR HAIR ON/Office life/ Busy timetables

Complete the story by choosing the correct sentence from the list above

Preferring observation to conversation, Angela stood by the buffet table, (________) (I) and soaking up the congenial atmosphere of the cocktail party. A little get-together (_______), indeed! (I) To think of all the extra hours, the anxiety, the frustrations, the emergency meetings, the last minute hiring of extra staff: (_______) deserved a little celebration! (I) All those who had participated in the project were there, and the (_______) was excellent (I). She herself had spent hours organising the event, (_______) (I), written and (_______) (I) complete with (_______) (I). She had done a jolly good job too, and to see a happy smile on everybody's face was quite a relief. A few steps away, Rafael was recycling one of his best one-liners and being his entertaining self again, which, with (_______) of late (IV), hadn't happened in a long while. Pete (_______) (IV), but showed no sign of losing weight over it, as his shirt buttons were straining to hold in his girth. Abi had obviously stuck to the advice that "(_______)" and looked radiant (I). She talked excitedly, occasionally providing a sighting of her tongue stud.

The maitre d'O's voice cut through Angela's thoughts: "Can I tempt you to a delicious Scandinavian Ceviche?" Angela hesitated briefly and went for the smoked salmon chip instead, which she daintily took from the proffered plate. "We are getting (_______)" she said (II), "your catering team has laid on a sumptuous spread, which is (_______) (II), considering the deadline you had to work to, to say nothing of the last minute changes!" Arrangements had indeed been made at very short notice as news of the project director's departure had only been released ten days before. It had proved (_______) to the short time frame (I). But a celebratory evening without Amanda was out of the question of course, because without her there'd probably be nothing to celebrate at all! Rumours were flying thick and fast that she'd known of her dismissal for some time but had soldiered on as brightly as she could for the team's sake. Whether her successor would even see out six months was (________) (III). Not just one thing contributed to the general scepticism, but (________) (III), and now that they were (________) the next major stage in the project (III), the question was (________) (III)? This get-together was charged with more emotion than your average party. "Well, (________) Ms Croydon (II), our people have a very good record of delivering on customers' expectations! Before leaving, could you spare a few minutes to check through the estimate and sign it? We'll send the bill through to your accounts department. Uncorked champagne bottles won't be charged, as agreed". "Well, (________), would it (III), if we appeared to have OD'd on Champagne"? Conversation wasn't Angela's strong point, but she liked the easy, amiable chatter such occasions provided, the hum of happy conversation and cheerful banter.

Abi came up to her in full humming bird mode: "Angela, your glass is empty; I'll go and track us down some champagne, shall I? You aren't feeling lonely, are you?" "Distance lends enchantment to the view, Abi. How are you enjoying your evening, and what do you think of the setting?" "Actually, I quite like the minimalist design. The (________) shades of brown and light green (I) is quite stylish, don't you think? I could pick up a few decorating tips myself! Well, perfect evening, anyway! All credit to the organiser! "Abi's voice trailed off as she made for the waiter who was wending his way through the crowd looking for a glass to replenish. "**The secret of success is preparation**, as we all know" Angela's words called after her.

AN OUNCE OF DISCRETION IS WORTH A POUND OF WIT

I - CLERICAL FUNCTIONS

parked up	CLERICAL/Travelling/ Arrival at the airport
on the other end	CLERICAL/Telephone/Landline
notice had been posted on	CLERICAL/Organising a seminar/ Transportation
procedural hoops she would have to jump through	CLERICAL/Operating procedures/ Workflow
bumped off his agenda	CLERICAL/Organising a seminar/ Ins and outs of the day's agenda

II - TALKING THE TALK

By some miracle of scheduling	TALKING THE TALK/Being positive/ Looking at the bright side

IV - KEEP YOUR HAIR ON

go above and beyond	KEEP YOUR HAIR ON/Polite and not so polite pointers
wouldn't go amiss	KEEP YOUR HAIR ON/Polite and not so polite pointers
it devolved on her	KEEP YOUR HAIR ON/Office Life/ Job description
and up with an unmanageable backlog	KEEP YOUR HAIR ON/Office Life/ Busy timetables
Let me just grab a pen I'll jot it down	KEEP YOUR HAIR ON/Office Life/ On the office premises

...➤

slip down on her list of priorities	KEEP YOUR HAIR ON/Office Life/ Organisational skill
just as she was about to	KEEP YOUR HAIR ON/Office Life/ Job description
Once she'd kicked off all these things, she would need to see them through	KEEP YOUR HAIR ON/Office Life/ Busy timetable

Complete the story by choosing the correct sentence from the list above

Whatever Ruth was going to say next was stilled. An A4 (_______) her office door (I) and she caught sight of it (_______) fish her key out of her pocket (IV) while turning the corner of the corridor. She immediately felt a pang of apprehension. Emergency wasn't out of the run of her duties, but this felt very odd. Despite the block letters, she could tell the message had been scribbled by Fiona, and as Ruth was letting the full meaning of its content sink in, the phone started ringing behind the door. "Theo's laptop stolen, more later. Please see to arrangements". She managed to pick up before the fourth ring activated her answering machine. So much for my once-in-a-while leisurely after lunch coffee, she thought to herself as she heard Fiona's voice (_______) (I). "(_______): 37363, and she's the site manager's assistant, ok, thanks (IV). I know, I have no idea where to start myself! I can't begin to imagine the number of things that will have to be (_______) if he is to be without access to all his files (I). I'll call him, right away, and find out more. Talk later". It turned out that Theo's laptop and the bag that contained it, along with the passports and car keys, had disappeared while the International removal van was (_______) in front of his new house (I). In the heat of the action, it had been left unattended, the consequences of which were hard to appraise at this stage, but they certainly involved acquiring a new company computer and a SecurID. This in turn meant furnishing the head of site with the exact circumstances of the theft in order to establish the risks of data piracy and fraud. Ruth knew this was only the beginning. Among all the things she had planned on doing in the next couple of days, some items would have to (_______) (IV); especially if the embassy had to be called for a new passport, with all the (_______) and the waiting time (I). Endless forms to be filled, police records to be faxed, the right people to be contacted, an appointment with the garage for a new lock to be filled, Theo's senior manager to be appraised of his recent misfortune. (_______) (IV) and God knows how long that was going to take. Meanwhile, of course, her in-box would keep building up and she'd (_______) to see to the most urgent requests (IV). The last thing she wanted was to (_______) (IV), but (_______) to make sure everything went back to normal as soon as possible (IV). That was going to be today's and tomorrow's priority.

(_______), no major event was on the cards in the next few days, except for the following morning's conference (II). Theo did have access to his Outlook calendar but since he'd hardly had time to draw breath because of the day's events, he would probably need reminding. A few directions to get to the venue (_______) either (IV). Ruth reflected that the circumstances of the computer's disappearance were best kept secret and that her first instincts to keep the whole thing quiet were right. If Fiona and her bunch were to know more, she might as well have taken out a full page announcement on next month's Newsletter. That could only reflect badly on her boss. **An ounce of discretion is worth a pound of wit.**

STRENGTH IN NUMBERS

I - CLERICAL FUNCTIONS

the transport system had collapsed.	CLERICAL/Travelling/Transport and Timing
firm up the plans so that she could book the flight	CLERICAL/Travelling/Thinking ahead
one well-placed call can save a lot of hassle	CLERICAL/Telephone/Landline
things that were running her late	CLERICAL/Timetables and meetings/ Duration of an appointment
everything checked out	CLERICAL/Travelling/Adjustments
no loose ends.	CLERICAL/Travelling/Adjustments
arrange the car service pickup time	CLERICAL/Travelling/Adjustments
traffic had been at a standstill	CLERICAL/Travelling/Transport and Timing
having an early finish	CLERICAL/Time/Créneaux horaires/ Horaires
motorists were getting nowhere fast	CLERICAL/Travelling/Transport and Timing
wrapped up the details	CLERICAL/Organising a seminar/ Conference material
Due to the high volume of calls,	CLERICAL/Telephone/Landline

II - TALKING THE TALK

as I normally expect from you	TALKING THE TALK/Being positive/Praising people
was the snow lying	TALKING THE TALK/ Facilitators/The weather
"I'll put my mind to it"	TALKING THE TALK/ Facilitators/The ready word

···➤

Going outside chilled you to the bone	TALKING THE TALK/ Facilitators/The weather

III- A PHRASE A DAY

This is an excellent rundown,	A PHRASE A DAY/Staying power/ Pressure

IV- KEEP YOUR HAIR ON

"It's high time we pushed off"	KEEP YOU HAIR ON/Office Life/ Time spent during the office day
it would hang over her	KEEP YOU HAIR ON/Office Life/ Busy timetables
slew of e-mails	KEEP YOU HAIR ON/Office Life/ Busy timetables
look in on	KEEP YOU HAIR ON/Office Life/On the office premises
contract to track down	KEEP YOU HAIR ON/Office Life/ Job description

Complete the story by choosing the correct sentence from the list above

Amy was running her fingers round the edge of her folder, politely waiting for her turn to talk to Susanna, and hoping that she'd come in on the tail end of her conversation with Chris. In view of Susanna's upcoming trip back to the US, they needed to (______) shortly (I), and (______) accordingly (I). While waiting, Amy mentally reviewed all the (______) (I), the (______) she was left with (IV); Susanna's appointment with Sam to reschedule; David's hiring (______) (IV); Dawn's request for a Blackberry. She was becoming mildly impatient. A shaft of sunlight came in the window illuminating millions of specks of dust and providing a welcome break from the dull light of a wintry day. Chris pulled out a chair for Amy, thus signalling that his conversation with Susanna was over and made his way out, calling (_______), Susanna" (II). Amy had been tempted to sidle out, but unless she dealt with Susanna's journey today, (_______) until it was done (IV). They (_______) of the trip in five minutes flat (I), and Amy left, satisfied that (_______) (I) and there were (_______) (I).

The morning went by, as busy as ever. On the only rare occasions when Amy got out of her seat, she stole a look out of the window. With her thumb and forefinger, she inched apart the pale grey slats of the ropey Venetian blind. (_______) (II), as she'd realised coming in to work that morning, and now, it was almost as if snow was on its way. Something had been niggling her since mid-morning, and unconsciously caused her to prick up her ears once in a while: it wasn't as if her colleagues ever had any shortage of things to do, so why did the place feel so unusually quiet? She'd heard of no major event that would keep them away from their offices that particular day. Across the partition, she could hear Susanna complimenting her interlocutor:" (_______) (III), (_______) (II), could you forward it to Chris as well?"

And then, it all came back to her; the first snowflakes she caught sight of triggered it. Already there was a light dusting of snow on the ground and memories of last year's gridlock came rushing back to her. Within hardly an hour, (_______) (I) and (_______) (I). Of course, living and working in Massachusetts, Susanna was unlikely to be fazed by a few snowflakes. Amy picked up the phone and called reception. Romain's familiar voice came: "Sorry, Ms Bird, there's no way I can reserve a taxi for you. (_______) (I), taxi companies are simply overwhelmed and aren't taking anymore customers". Amy's hunch was confirmed. The sooner she got back and safe to her hotel in Paris, the better. She looked up the Mappy driving directions map on the internet. The whole Paris area was a tangle of red lines: (________) obviously (I), and Susanna's 30 minute drive back might well turn out to be twice or three times as long. A firm believer in the notion that (________) (I), Amy decided that her next move was to turn to Mr Oliveira, her own trusted taxi driver. No luck there either. She was running short of options, and now not only (________) (II), but it was snowing heavily. The kind of landscape that would have had the company Artists Club's budding painters reaching out for their paintbrushes, but which was sure to make life very difficult for workers who were (________) (I).

Amy even thought of calling Daserole drivers across the Atlantic, hoping against hope that because of their extensive network, they might oblige. As a matter of fact she did –to no avail. Time had passed, it was already past 4 pm; the few remaining colleagues had left in dribs and drabs. Amy pictured herself walking back to the station, up the steep, slippery slope and then on the crammed Paris RER and metro because she couldn't possibly leave her to brave them with so little practice of both the underground and the language!

But then, Kim showed up and Thomas, and Vinona, and Jonathan. They were coming out of a meeting and about to (________) Susanna (IV). (________) (IV), one of them said, "they'll have to helicopter us out of here if we aren't careful". Amy sneaked looks at Susanna's low heel court shoes, unsure that they were well suited for cutting through new snow. But she was breathing a little more easily now. As the party were trudging their way up the slope to the RER station, a happy bunch of revellers who threatened to slip at every step and whose slightly excited voices echoed in the stilled, silent street, she couldn't help thinking that some people would pay good money to see this. **Strength in numbers** indeed!

GENTLENESS IS NOT WEAKNESS BUT RESTRAINED STRENGTH

I - CLERICAL FUNCTIONS

be roped into	CLERICAL/Timetables and meetings/ Starter points/Appointments

II - TALKING THE TALK

frame it all with more positive news	TALKING THE TALK/Being positive/ Remaining positive in spite of small hiccups

III - A PHRASE A DAY

had a ringside seat throughout its development	A PHRASE A DAY/ Clearsightedness/Direction
an emotive issue	A PHRASE A DAY/ Communication/Public relations
was going to be a high wire act	A PHRASE A DAY/Miscellaneous/ Achievements and Know-how
fan the flames	A PHRASE A DAY/ Taking a stance/Conflict
be led away from their goal	A PHRASE A DAY/ Clearsightedness/Direction
got on the wrong side	A PHRASE A DAY/Miscellaneous/ Individuals
chart a steady course through	A PHRASE A DAY/Staying power/ Pressure
dodged the question	A PHRASE A DAY/Exerting an influence/Manipulation
was in for the long haul	A PHRASE A DAY/ Clearsightedness/Direction

•••➤

the living embodiment of its history	A PHRASE A DAY/ Clearsightedness/Direction
cutting losses	A PHRASE A DAY/Strategy/ Medium and long-term planning
reinforcing the company's claim on the future	A PHRASE A DAY/Strategy/ Medium and long-term planning
Head Honcho	A PHRASE A DAY/Miscellaneous/ Hierarchy
constant carping	A PHRASE A DAY/ Taking a stance/Conflict
a real kick in the teeth	A PHRASE A DAY/Exerting an influence/Influencing others
he'd caught the mood of the assembly	A PHRASE A DAY/ Communication/Public relations
defused a potentially severe crisis	A PHRASE A DAY/ Communication/Public relations
the hardest hit	A PHRASE A DAY/ Taking a stance/Conflict
be fighting their own corner	A PHRASE A DAY/ Taking a stance/Conflict

IV - KEEP YOUR HAIR ON

I certainly need a caffeine boost	KEEP YOUR HAIR ON/ Polite and not so polite pointers

Complete the story by choosing the correct sentence from the list above

His "Good morning" was a mere whisper. As he walked past Abigail's office, Remy was lost in thought; and by the look of him, sleep hadn't visited him the night before. Just now he was quietly cursing that he'd let himself (_______) this personnel representative job (I). He felt it fell to him to inform his colleagues of the impending closure of their Paris site. Much as he would have liked to (_______) (II), the prospects were pretty grim. For many, it was going to be (_______) (III). "Fancy a cup of coffee?" inquired Abigail, motioning him to the coffee machine. Remy forced a smile and introduced a positive tone into his voice. "(_______) this morning (IV). Can't say no to a cup of coffee!" How could the management be so dismissive of the people at the receiving end of this major restructuring plan? How could they so blatantly tread on people's sensibilities like they did? It was bound to be (_______) and his would be an uphill task (III). First breaking the news – as long as nothing transpired before, and then negotiating with the trade-unions over the coming redundancy payments. That (_______) (III). Not to mention the evening out with the top management scheduled for the following week. Remy had two crucial messages to pass on to them, which they might not be prepared to hear. And of course, it would be in nobody's interest if he (_______) of them (III). "I was thinking, Remy, about our next company trip: how about we made some inquiries about Borneo as our next destination?" Abigail was asking as he fell into step beside her. "What about it indeed?" Remy thought glumly. "We've had two cancellations for our coming weekend in Prague, haven't we?" Remy was pleased he'd (_______), and, changing the subject, steamed right on with the conversation (III).

In the face of an industrial dispute this big, Remy's resources were finite. But he knew his contribution in the transition process could be significant. The restructuring wasn't about figures or about (_______) (III) while (_______) (III): it was about men and women whose livelihood was taken away from them and who were now vulnerable to the uncertainties of a ruthless job market. They would need both time and paycheques that would free them from financial worries for a while. Those were the two messages he would relay to the (______) when he'd be visiting next week (III). His twenty-five years in the company had made him (______) (III). He'd (______) (III) and now he was lead actor in its final act.

That Tuesday afternoon, Remy did face up to his new responsibilities. His stomach in knots and mindful that he had to tread carefully, he imparted the news that closure was imminent and that those who wouldn't be able to move to the new site in Strasburg were out of a job. Thankfully (______) (III); he could feel he had (______) (III). Emotions shouldn't cloud their judgement, including his, and they shouldn't (______), which was that each single employee should get the best deal (III).

Responses to the news were bound to vary. With the size of his severance package and so close to retirement, Dominique would soon think all his Christmases had come home at once. Laura on the other hand, with her husband on the dole and her three children, would be among (______) (III). There'd be the token moaners and their (______) (III); those who'd (______) indifferent to the interests of their colleagues (III); those who would be only too pleased to (______) discontent (III). Now he (______) (III) and in the months ahead he'd have to (______) troubled times indeed (III). He had embraced his mission with a not inconsiderable display of brainpower, but also with great empathy and tact. **Gentleness**, he knew, **is not weakness but restrained strength**.

LIFE IS EITHER DARING ADVENTURE OR NOTHING

I - CLERICAL FUNCTIONS

signed in on arrival	CLERICAL/Organising a seminar/ Organising/List of participants
well in advance would allow for	CLERICAL/Travelling/ Travel arrangements/ Transport and Timing
a sign with his name on it for easy identification	CLERICAL/Travelling/ Arrival at airport/Signage
meeting and greeting	CLERICAL/Travelling/ Arrival at airport/Signage
had gone ahead in spite of the short notice	CLERICAL/Timetables and meetings/Confirmation
to push key items off the agenda	CLERICAL/Organising a seminar/ The ins and outs of the day's agenda
arrived a full hour before Megumi and Hoshi were due	CLERICAL/Difficulties in setting up an appointment
wrap up at 4 o'clock sharp	CLERICAL/Organising a seminar/ The ins and outs of the day's agenda
his visa would run out	CLERICAL/Travelling/Travel arrangements/Thinking ahead
It's all going to time	CLERICAL/Time/Créneaux horaires/Horaires
sit in traffic on the périphérique	CLERICAL/Travelling/ Travel arrangements/ Transport and Timing
Charlotte's best bet	CLERICAL/Travelling/ Arrival at airport/Procedures

···➤

II - TALKING THE TALK	
you're a gem	TALKING THE TALK/Being positive/ Praising people
there wouldn't be enough gold stars in the world	TALKING THE TALK/Being positive/ Praising people
IV - KEEP YOUR HAIR ON	
what did his last servant die of	KEEP YOUR HAIR ON/ Polite and not so polite pointers
I'm going out of the door as we speak	KEEP YOU HAIR ON/Office Life/ Office premises
was called up	KEEP YOU HAIR ON/Office Life/ Word processing

Complete the story by choosing the correct sentence from the list above

A Land rover pulled out of a space, opening up a choice parking spot for Greg. He swerved into it, cranked up the handbrake and killed the engine. He was well ahead of himself, he knew, and had (______) (I). At least, arriving (______) whatever time was needed to get to the arrival hall (I), and negotiate the labyrinthine Terminal II multi-storey underground car park. "Hi, Charlotte! (______)" (I), he shouted into his mobile phone as he picked his way through the milling crowd. "I was expecting to (______) to Charles de Gaulle (I), but it was free-flowing all the way". "You know what Neil McElroy said about airports?" Charlotte replied in her not unusual playful tone, "In the space age, man will be able to go around the world in two hours – one hour for flying and one hour to get to the airport. It seems you've beaten the record! Call me as soon as you've picked them up, we may have a few loose ends to tie up". Greg was used to gadding about airports, but (_______) foreign guests (I), and holding (_______) was a first (I)! He was now absently watching the passengers drifting out of the arrival area, mentally rehearsing his schedule for the next two days and a half. Once he'd collected the two Japanese delegates, they'd be driving off directly to the company's headquarters, south of the capital, hoping to catch Olivier's opening speech in time.

The seminar (_______) (I). They'd had to (_______) due to the extremely tight timetable (I), and would have to (_______) on the Friday (I), in time for the participants to taxi back to the airport –well, for those who had to fly back home, that is. The comforting thought was that he wouldn't be roped in to do the driving! Greg's phone trilled at the bottom of his inside jacket pocket. He rummaged for it and took Charlotte's call. As he did so, his parking ticket fell out. He picked it up and mechanically ran his eyes over the small print before putting it back in his pocket: Roissy, 30/03/11 A 11:45:53. "Greg", Charlotte was saying, (_______) (IV) and locking my office. Olivier says I'm needed at the HQ. I did tell him I was on a sun lounger, sipping Martinis and he'd have to wait, but he just pretended not to take the hint. Honestly, Greg, (_______) (IV)?! How about we beam him up and run the seminar without him? "Oh, come on Charlotte, (_______), you know that (II). You've done a great job organising the seminar. If it weren't for this irrepressible sense of humour of yours, (_______) (II)! Greg's two guests were duly collected. No battles with parking meters to be fought, no traffic hold-ups. They were at the location on time, (_______) (I) and were immediately caught in the whirlwind of activities, plenary meetings, workshops, discussion groups. The fine balance between work and recreation was achieved, the food was excellent, the hotel arrangements perfect.

On the Friday morning just after breakfast, the fifty delegates trickled back into the main room and resumed their seats. They were still busy chatting, rebooting their computers, or already poring over graphics and data bases when a message (________) on the central screen for everyone to read (IV). One by one, they looked up at it. The gentle hum of conversation soon broke into a buzz of excitement as the full meaning of the notice sank in. All heads were angled up now, transfixed by the message. The news was just plain bad. Frédérique was cursing under her breath that this would only enhance France's poor image as a strike-prone country, Tjhin was worried that (________) (I) and started fretting about his return to Indonesia. As for poor Greg, he couldn't believe he was in for a two-hour drive back to the airport yet again!

This is how it read:

WARNING NOTICE

The union of taxi drivers has called a strike and is taking industrial action over poor working conditions.

Transportation to both airports and train stations will therefore be severely disrupted today.

A. Members of the team will offer car sharing services to Paris Charles de Gaulle. See list.

B. For other destinations, local shopkeepers have come forward and offered to put their vans and pickups at our disposal. Those of you who need transportation are requested to contact the baker's, the grocer's and fishmonger's (today of all days). We are doing our utmost to make this alternative solution foolproof.

A smile flickered across Olivier's set expression; he had obviously worked out the clues and immediately seen through the hoax. Unperturbed he went on tapping away at his laptop. Meanwhile there was great commotion. Charlotte sidled out of the building, a little dazed at the impact of her April Fool day's prank and slightly overwhelmed by how well it had caught on.

When she came back in, and resumed her seat next to Tjhin, he leant forward and, as if letting her in on a little secret he said: "It's a joke, it's a joke. There isn't a strike!!"

Upholding tradition was commendable, but maybe not (________) (I)! On the other hand, "**Life is either daring adventure or nothing**", she felt sure. She'd obviously chosen the former.

WHEN SOMETHING IS WORTH DOING, IT'S WORTH DOING WELL

I - CLERICAL FUNCTIONS

I'm not yet signed in on all the systems	CLERICAL/Operating procedures/ Workflow
I've had it with printers jamming	CLERICAL/Glitches
on the blink	CLERICAL/Glitches
on sick leave	CLERICAL/Difficulties in setting up an appointment/Busy schedules

II - TALKING THE TALK

If there are specific areas that you wish to be involved in, please let me know	TALKING THE TALK/HR and communication/Job Description
win you a few Brownie points	TALKING THE TALK/Being positive/ Appreciation of hard work
make headway	TALKING THE TALK/Being positive/ Looking on the bright side
Her time commitment to the works council must have been considerable	TALKING THE TALK/Mapping out the future/Planning ahead
redirect the request to another number	TALKING THE TALK/Connecting people/Acting as an intermediary
fill me in on	TALKING THE TALK/Connecting people/Acting as an intermediary
which is a step up from when I arrived	TALKING THE TALK/Being positive/ Looking on the bright side
she'd grow into the job	TALKING THE TALK/Being positive/ Looking on the bright side

III - A PHRASE A DAY

had her work cut out	A PHRASE A DAY/Staying power/ Persistence
get out there and do what had to be done	A PHRASE A DAY/Staying power/ Persistence
she got her bearings in the maze of	A PHRASE A DAY/ Clearsightedness/Direction
she could puzzle out the details	A PHRASE A DAY/Being methodical/Short term planning
in the driving seat on the market	A PHRASE A DAY/Miscellaneous/ Our place on the scene of World Affairs
an important plank in the company's networking strategy	A PHRASE A DAY/Strategy/ Medium and long-term planning

IV - KEEP YOUR HAIR ON

start ticking tasks off	KEEP YOUR HAIR ON/ Organisational skills
wouldn't come amiss	KEEP YOUR HAIR ON/ Polite and not so polite pointers
achieve some measure of order	KEEP YOUR HAIR ON/ Polite and not so polite pointers
the cupboards had been turned out	KEEP YOU HAIR ON/Office Life/ Removals
there wasn't a spare surface anywhere	KEEP YOU HAIR ON/Office Life/ Removals
her mental to-do list into shape	KEEP YOUR HAIR ON/Office life/ Organisational skills
have come in from your site via the internal post	KEEP YOU HAIR ON/Office Life/ On the premises

Complete the story by choosing the correct sentence from the list provided

Hillary's head lifted slowly into view from behind her desk, as she heard a booming voice cut through the hushed silence of the corridor. She'd been squatting there, out of sight for the past half hour methodically sorting the content of her drawers into piles and trying to (_______) in her new office (IV). "(_______) (I)! How long has this one been (_______), Hilla… Blimey, Hillary! Is this some kind of war zone (I)?" Matthew froze as he was about to come in the door. Boxes were stacked in piles on top of the desk, loose files were strewn over the window ledge waiting to be sorted, (_______) (IV) and (_______) (IV)! As a temping assistant, she'd been the interim owner of quite a few offices, but none had ever required such drastic action as Claudia's. "(_______)" was one comment she could remember from her interview with the company's Human Resources director (II). Spring cleaning on that scale was certainly not the kind of "area" that would immediately come to mind. "Mr McGuire", she said pleasantly, "it all comes down to the theory of maximum usage of available space". Hillary had only known her colleague sales manager a couple of days, so she played it safe and called him by his surname. "Well, you'll be lucky if you're done before the end of the week, Hillary, but this is sure to (_______) (II)! Good move!" Six weeks after Claudia had left (_______) (I), her office had very conveniently become multipurpose: a depot for office supplies, a General delivery address holding unsorted mail for almost the entire floor, a storeroom for contracts awaiting signature or pending archiving, a haven for lost keys, and much more. Hillary could have sworn, all important knowledge on tourism, travel operators and Company Package holidays was in there too! The sheer size of travel-related literature accumulated over the company's lifetime was mind-boggling: backup issues of travel catalogues; quotes from travel agencies; correspondence with group travel organisers; postcards. Hillary obviously (_______) (III). Wasn't her only option to (_______) (III)? Now that she'd got (_______) (IV), she could (_______) (III) and (_______) (II).Besides, no one on the team seemed to have planned on making time to introduce her to the job – a common enough pattern. The "lull before the storm" syndrome, as she knew all too well.

Hillary disappeared behind the desk again. The phone went off; she jumped to her feet, half expecting the call to be yet another query about a forthcoming trip to some faraway place or about season tickets for the Paris Opera House. Claudia was, by the look of it, the company's de facto travel agent. (_______) (II)! Hillary picked up. "Hillary Jones, Tazina & Co, can I help?" She gave a quick sideways look at her notes on how to operate her VoIP phone, in case she'd have to (_______) (II). "Hi, Nathaly! Glad you're calling. Yes! The contracts (_______) (IV). I have followed your instructions to the letter. Isabelle still has to (_______) what to do next, but everything is under control (II). Actually, there's been improvement since we last spoke: the technician's called in, he's configured my computer, (_______) (II); it's now connected to the printer – not that it does much good since it seems to have a mind of its own. Nope! ERP Software not accessible, (_______) (I). It will come in good time, I know! Ok, Nathaly, bye for now!"

Sitting crossed-legged on her swivel chair and staring out of the window into the middle distance, Hillary drummed her fingers on her chin. It would be some time before (_______) complex contract procedures and regulations (III). But (_______) soon enough (II). Once the basics were in place, (_______) as she went along (III). That's what temping was all about. She worked her shoulders around. "My back's killing me" she said aloud. As if on cue, Matthew knocked at her open door. "Tea, coffee?" he said. Hillary turned round, a lock of hair spilling into her face. "A nice cup of tea (________) (IV)!" Michael and Gaetan joined them and they were soon deep in conversation in front of the coffee machine on the ground floor. They were on first-name terms by now too. The event in Brussels which all the team attended – and the reason behind the deserted offices and hushed atmosphere on floor 1 – was a must. The company was (________) worldwide (III), but in an age of social media, events like this one remained (________) (III). "Anyway, Hillary, when they're back they won't believe their eyes. You seem to be doing a great job of tidying up Claudia's office! "Hillary felt the corners of her mouth turning up in a pleased smile. She liked it when people heaped the extra praise on her.

By the end of the week, all the team members were hovering by her office door, peeking a look inside now that it was in apple pie order and fit for purpose. **When something is worth doing, it's worth doing well**.

EVEN THE BEST LAID PLANS CAN GO AWRY

I - CLERICAL FUNCTIONS

I'll give you a shout	CLERICAL/Timetables and meetings/ Starters points/Offering-requesting a service
flexibility in choosing a date was bound to be very limited	CLERICAL/Timetables and meetings/ Difficulties in setting up an appointment/Busy schedules
scan her pass across the reader for the glass doors to slide open	CLERICAL/Operating procedures/ Passes
at such short notice	CLERICAL/Clerical functions/Timetables and meetings/Confirmation
Profuse apologies	CLERICAL/Timetables and meetings/ Difficulties in setting up an appointment/Apologies for a late reply
allow sufficient time for the catering team to get from one end of the site to the other	CLERICAL/Timetables and meetings/ Starters points/Coordinating an appointment
set up a date	CLERICAL/Timetables and meetings/ Recurring meetings
would be solidly booked	CLERICAL/Timetables and meetings/ Difficulties in setting up an appointment/Busy schedules
tying up loose ends	CLERICAL/Travelling/Travel arrangements/Adjustments
time was romping away	CLERICAL/Timetables and meetings/ Difficulties in setting up an appointment/Busy schedules
double book a room	CLERICAL/Telephone/Teleconferences
made a beeline for	CLERICAL/Organising a seminar/ The ins and outs of the day's agenda

ensure the smooth running of	CLERICAL/Holidays
Please note that the drinks party will now be held in room K 006	CLERICAL/Events/Invitations
were back on track	CLERICAL/Seminars/ The ins and outs of the day's agenda
She had fallen behind with her work	CLERICAL/Glitches
People were counting on her to pass on vital and timely information	CLERICAL/Operating procedures/ Requests/Transportation
posted on the meeting room doors	CLERICAL/Seminars/Organising/ Transportation

II - TALKING THE TALK

this wasn't going to be an easy switch to make	TALKING THE TALK/Clarifying
glad they had everything squared away	ALKING THE TALK/Clarifying
how indebted to them she was for	TALKING THE TALK/Being positive/ Appreciation of hard work

III - A PHRASE A DAY

It was all systems go	A PHRASE A DAY/Dynamics
against all odds	A PHRASE A DAY/Staying power/Persistence

IV - KEEP YOUR HAIR ON

in preparation for a busy next few days	KEEP ON HAIR ON/Office Life/ Busy timetables
make headway with	KEEP ON HAIR ON/Office Life/ Busy timetables
ticking tasks off	KEEP ON HAIR ON/Office Life/ Organisational skills

Complete the story by choosing the correct sentence from the list provided

Sarah stormed out of her office, and (_______) the front door (I). She ran down the two flights of stairs outside the building, taking the steps two at a time, sprinted along the flower beds in the courtyard, halted in her tracks to (_______) (I), passed reception and arrived gasping for breath at the catering manager's office. "You don't mean that the whole thing is off?" she blurted trying to keep the quiver out of her voice as she enquired, and glad her breathlessness served to cover her confusion. "I can't think of any alternative, Mrs Dean", came the reply, "there is just no venue for the drinks party to be held, especially (_______)" (I). Mr Devere was obviously affecting a composure that he didn't feel: the amount of splendid food going to waste, the staff resources allocated to hosting the party and the refund that he was unlikely to obtain in full, were no exciting prospect. "(_______) (I), Mr Devere, I do appreciate this is a major inconvenience. There's got to be a way, surely." This wasn't Sarah's finest hour, she should have known better than to (_______) (I). Mr Devere's phone call, five minutes earlier, hadn't half brought her up with a jolt! "Where did you say we were to lay out the food and drink, Mrs Dean?" he'd asked, "the place is taken up with a meeting all day." Despite her protestations about having done things by the rule book and to the place being booked in her name, Sarah was in for more disappointment and embarrassment. "Your reservation's been approved by R-Scheduler all right, but apparently it is made out for October next year, Mrs Dean, not October of this year!"

Sarah remembered how unusually and inexplicably easy it had been to (_______) for today's lunchtime party (I). The site was due to close before end of year and as building after building was emptied out, space was at a premium: even weeks ahead of the event all the available rooms (________) (I) and (________) (I). Well, it all made sense now. It said something for her scrupulous nature that Sarah had spent the hours leading up to the event checking on responses to the invitation, contacting the catering team to make sure everything would be delivered in quantity and on time, and generally (________) (I). Never in a month of Sundays would she have anticipated such an oversight!

Now, (________) (I), and there wasn't the slightest shadow of a solution in sight. "How about using the cafeteria?" Sarah offered. But this was immediately ruled out as the only available space was already spoken for. Both could see (________) (II). Mr Devere's level tone belied his anxiety. "I'll make a phone call", he said decisively, "see if I can get the keys to building K. It's completely unfurnished, but I could get the maintenance team to bring in a few tables. That might do the trick. We'd have to (________), of course, and several trips, but at least it's worth a try (I). (________) as soon as I know more (I)." Sarah bared her teeth in as broad a smile as she could possibly muster, and thanked him abundantly.

As soon as she got confirmation that Mr Devere's idea was going ahead, she typed up a short text. It read "(________)" (I) and was sent as an update to all participants. She printed out two paper versions of the same, to be (________) (I) so that straying partiers would be redirected to the right location. The time was now approaching 12.30 and movement in the courtyard signalled that preparations for the cocktail were under way. (________) (III). Sarah sat back in her swivel chair, lacing her fingers behind her head and breathing a sigh of relief at how things (________) now that the crisis was over (I). (________) somewhat (I), having had to leave aside matters related to the department's impending move. (________) (I): the selective sorting of office documents, and the practical guidelines to (_______) the transition (I). How to tag items of office equipment was equally important. In order for them to be safely routed to the new offices they must be reliably identified and properly labelled. She still had the afternoon ahead of her to follow up on the headphones. Now that most team members were going to work in open plan work spaces, they would be vital. Sarah was (_______) (II). She could go back to (_______) (IV) and (_______) her list of to-do things as long as your arm (_______) (IV). But just now, she was setting finger to keyboard again, typing a huge "Thank You' in brightly coloured Word Art letters. They would be accompanying the box of chocolates she was determined to buy Mr Devere and his team as a token of (_______) (II) making the drinks party happen (_______) (III). **Even the best laid plans can go awry.** Forming a real partnership can go a long way towards making them work, though, and as a matter of fact, had saved the day.

AN IDEA IS WORTHLESS UNLESS YOU USE IT

I - CLERICAL FUNCTIONS

Given the short timeframe	CLERICAL/Timetables/Starter points
back to back meetings	CLERICAL/Timetables/Being tactful
be put on hold	CLERICAL/Timetables/Difficulties in setting up an appointment
there were no loose ends	CLERICAL/Travelling/Travel arrangements
made for easy identification	CLERICAL/Travelling/Meeting and greeting/Signage
round everybody up for a good photo shoot	CLERICAL/Seminars/Organising/Photos
the meeting had been kept moving on schedule	CLERICAL/Organising a seminar/Ins and outs of a day's agenda
felt a little out of her depth	CLERICAL/Organising a seminar/Conference material
hard slog and dedication	CLERICAL/Events/Invitations
there was no seating plan	CLERICAL/Events/At the restaurant
speeding up the purchase request approval	CLERICAL/Operating procedures
get it past the financial controller	CLERICAL/Operating procedures

II - TALKING THE TALK

The catering team, which was more than professional	TALKING THE TALK/Being positive/Appreciation of hard work
was taking shape nicely	TALKING THE TALK/Being positive/Looking on the bright side
had gone without a hitch	TALKING THE TALK/Being positive/Looking on the bright side
very medicated	TALKING THE TALK/Facilitators/Health

III - A PHRASE A DAY

she had sat in on	A PHRASE A DAY/Taking stock/Facts
had achieved its stated objectives and then some	A PHRASE A DAY/Taking stock/ Successes
kicked into the long grass	A PHRASE A DAY/Taking stock/ Failures
take some doing	A PHRASE A DAY/ Exerting an influence/Persuasion
needed a shot in the arm	A PHRASE A DAY/Dynamics/ On the move
boost the energy levels	A PHRASE A DAY/Dynamics/ On the move

IV - KEEP YOUR HAIR ON

like herding cats	KEEP YOUR HAIR ON/Polite and not so polite pointers
she'd done twice her usual stint	KEEP YOUR HAIR ON/Office Life/Busy timetables
could freewheel a little	KEEP YOUR HAIR ON/Office Life/Busy timetables

Complete the story by choosing the correct sentence from the list above

Delegates from three continents had converged on that tiny little village, a mere dot on the map of the Greater Paris region. The « Domaine de Besalbel », was in the middle of nowhere, but offered its hosts remarkable surroundings, which, it was hoped, would make for a successful two days of both team building and high powered working sessions. After almost a year of (______) to the new project (I), the teams badly (______) (III) and this seminar aimed to (______) of all those so deeply involved in the project (III). Phone conversations, Web meetings and video-conferencing, were put on hold for a while, and virtual collaboration (______) (III) – for the duration, that is. Group dynamics, building trust and defining roles and goals were the order of the day. At this late point in the afternoon of 30 January Kirsty was running through her colour-coded to-do list. She was making sure (______) (I), aware that (______) lately (IV) but satisfied that everything (______) (II), and refusing to bow to pressure. One item highlighted in green read: list-for-lift-to-airport. This could (______) until Friday morning (I), ahead of the mid afternoon finish, she thought. "Ms Ferguson, glad you made it early! I take it the rest of the party will be here shortly? We still have concerns that we haven't received your payment yet: I'm afraid there's still no sign of a credit transfer on our account. We are way past the deadline'. Kirsty wrinkled her nose and let out a long-suffering sigh. Just when she thought she (______) (IV), bang went her peaceful ten minutes alone! The subject had given rise to some prickly conversation between her and her company's accountant. (______) (I), Kirsty had enquired about (______) (I), hoping to (______) swiftly (I) and duly settle the bill. Delays in payment reflected poorly on the company and compromised future bookings with the catering establishment. The owner was being diplomatic about it, but she could detect a trace of annoyance in his voice. Hardly a week before, his accountant had been far blunter and threatened to cancel the whole event, sending Kirsty into a spin of panic.

The two days were a success. (______), clearly had a hand in it (II). More generally, (______) (I), and the balance between intensive work and recreation was satisfactory. Some of the group building exercises produced the most hilarious songs and provided joyful moments; the food was superb; two of the outbuildings were steeped in history and had attracted a keen interest, and the bedrooms were sumptuous. The seminar (______) (III). Kirsty (______), of course, (I) since they were all blinding her with science, but judging from the sessions (______) (III), it had gone a long way towards relieving stress. Both the workshops and plenary meetings had helped clarifying roles, articulating longer-term goals and sharing observations and concerns. The furrowed eye-brows and worried expressions of some had now disappeared.

Apart from the trifling matter of Patricia Robinson's last minute request for an off-the-menu dish, everything (______) (II). Sam Bunn and Jaclyn had followed suit and been equally fussy with their food, but the catering team had kindly obliged. Kirsty thought that a fitting medium of respect for the staff's work wouldn't have gone amiss. She had, however, done a very good job of biting back a pointed remark. The badges (featuring the company's logo and colours) (______) (I), especially as (______) (I). Sadly, one badge had remained undelivered. Kirtsy reflected that it might, in fact, have been called the "Badge of Courage'. Its recipient had declined and stayed behind in Canada, (______) (II) and heroically struggling against her illness. "We all know how indebted we are to Pam and her role in our Project. How about sending her a little something saying how much she's being missed?" Michel had spoken into the mike; "I was thinking along the lines of a booklet with messages of good cheer and everybody's signature in it, together with a photograph? This means of course, that before Friday afternoon, we'll have to (______) (I)". The idea had instantly won wholehearted approval. For two days, writing pens and markers, glue sticks, coloured paper and card, self-stick coloured labels, and scissors were at people's disposal in the glassed-in seating area, off the main hall. Whether the delegates would stop by and indulge in a bit of handicraft was anybody's guess. Michel's idea had been ambitious: getting each and all to pause for a while in the course of their busy two days would certainly (________) (III). Pointing them in the direction of the improvised workshop would be very much (________) (IV). And yet, in spite of the (________) (I) and the overstretched timetable, people had been seen milling around the place. They were good humouredly giving their best shot at conveying their heartfelt sympathy and expressing their very best wishes to a dear colleague and friend. **An idea is worthless unless you use it.** Michel had used his and had done so advisedly. A Director of Human Resources with initiative.

KEY – CORRIGÉS

THE SECRET OF SUCCESS IS PREPARATION

Preferring observation to conversation, Angela stood by the buffet table, *nursing her drink* and soaking up the congenial atmosphere of the cocktail party. A little get-together *in recognition of everybody's hard work*, indeed! To think of all the extra hours, the anxiety, the frustrations, the emergency meetings, the last minute hiring of extra staff: *the team's accomplishments* deserved a little celebration! All those who had participated in the project were there, and the *turnout* was excellent. She herself had spent hours organising the event, *found a suitable place*, written and *sent out the invitations* complete with *a map giving travel directions*. She had done a jolly good job too, and to see a happy smile on everybody's face was quite a relief. A few steps away, Rafael was recycling one of his best one-liners and being his entertaining self again, which, with *all the work he had committed himself to* of late, hadn't happened in a long while. Pete *had been working himself to the bone*, but showed no sign of losing weight over it, as his shirt buttons were straining to hold in his girth. Abi had obviously stuck to the advice that "*you can never be overdressed for this kind of event*" and looked radiant. She talked excitedly, occasionally providing a sighting of her tongue stud.

The maitre d'O's voice cut through Angela's thoughts: "Can I tempt you to a delicious Scandinavian Ceviche?" Angela hesitated briefly and went for the smoked salmon chip instead, which she daintily took from the proffered plate. "We are getting *good feedback from our guests*" she said, "your catering team has laid on a sumptuous spread, which is *no mean feat*, considering the deadline you had to work to, to say nothing of the last minute changes!" Arrangements had indeed been made at very short notice as news of the project director's departure had only been released ten days before. It had proved *a juggle fitting everything in* to the short timeframe. But a celebratory evening without Amanda was out of the question of course, because without her there'd probably be nothing to celebrate at all! Rumours were flying thick and fast that she'd known of her dismissal for some time but had soldiered on as brightly as she could for the team's sake. Whether her successor would even see out six months was *a moot point*. Not just one thing contributed to the general scepticism, but *a whole set of circumstances*, and now that they were *a few removes from* the next major stage in the project, the question was *would the team sustain the pace*? This get-together was charged with more emotion than your average party. "Well, *all part of the service* Ms Croydon, our people have a very good record of delivering on customers' expectations! Before leaving, could you spare a few minutes to check through the estimate and sign it? We'll send the bill through to your accounts department. Uncorked champagne bottles won't be charged, as agreed". "Well, *it wouldn't look good*, would it, if we appeared to have OD'd on Champagne?" Conversation wasn't Angela's strong point, but she liked the easy, amiable chatter such occasions provided, the hum of happy conversation and cheerful banter.

Abi came up to her in full humming bird mode: "Angela, your glass is empty; I'll go and track us down some champagne, shall I? You aren't feeling lonely, are you?" "Distance lends enchantment to the view, Abi. How are you enjoying your evening, and what do you think of the setting?" "Actually, I quite like the minimalist design. The *colour scheme keyed to* shades of brown and light green is quite stylish, don't you think? I could pick up a few decorating tips myself! Well, perfect evening, anyway! All credit to the organiser!" Abi's voice trailed off as she made for the waiter who was wending his way through the crowd looking for a glass to replenish. "**The secret of success is preparation**, as we all know" Angela's words called after her.

AN OUNCE OF DISCRETION IS WORTH A POUND OF WIT

Whatever Ruth was going to say next was stilled. An A4 *notice had been posted on* her office door and she caught sight of it *just as she was about to* fish her key out of her pocket while turning the corner of the corridor. She immediately felt a pang of apprehension. Emergency wasn't out of the run of her duties, but this felt very odd. Despite the block letters, she could tell the message had been scribbled by Fiona, and as Ruth was letting the full meaning of its content sink in, the phone started ringing behind the door."Theo's laptop stolen, more later. Please see to arrangements". She managed to pick up before the fourth ring activated her answering machine. So much for my once-in-a-while leisurely after lunch coffee, she thought to herself as she heard Fiona's voice *on the other end. "Let me just grab a pen I'll jot it down*: 37363, and she's the site manager's assistant, ok, thanks. I know, I have no idea where to start myself! I can't begin to imagine the number of things that will have to be *bumped off his agenda* if he is to be without access to all his files. I'll call him, right away, and find out more. Talk later". It turned out that Theo's laptop and the bag that contained it, along with the passports and car keys, had disappeared while the International removal van was *parked up* in front of his new house. In the heat of the action, it had been left unattended, the consequences of which were hard to appraise at this stage, but they certainly involved acquiring a new company computer and an SecurID. This in turn meant furnishing the head of site with the exact circumstances of the theft in order to establish the risks of data piracy and fraud. Ruth knew this was only the beginning. Among all the things she had planned on doing in the next couple of days, some items would have to *slip down on her list of priorities*; especially if the embassy had to be called for a new passport, with all the *procedural hoops she would have to jump through* and the waiting time. Endless forms to be filled, police records to be faxed, the right people to be contacted, an appointment with the garage for a new lock to be fitted, Theo's senior manager to be appraised of his recent misfortune (...). *Once she'd kicked off all these things, she would need to see them through* and God knows how long that was going to take. Meanwhile, of course, her in-box would keep building up and she'd *go above and beyond* to see to the most urgent requests. The last thing she wanted was to *end up with an unmanageable backlog*, but *it devolved on her to* make sure everything went back to normal as soon as possible. That was going to be today's and tomorrow's priority.

By some miracle of scheduling, no major event was on the cards in the next few days, except for the following morning's conference. Theo did have access to his Outlook calendar but since he'd hardly had time to draw breath because of the day's events, he would probably need reminding. A few directions to get to the venue *wouldn't go amiss* either. Ruth reflected that the circumstances of the computer's disappearance were best kept secret and that her first instincts to keep the whole thing quiet were right. If Fiona and her bunch were to know more, she might as well have taken out a full page announcement on next month's Newsletter. That could only reflect badly on her boss. **An ounce of discretion is worth a pound of wit.**

STRENGTH IN NUMBERS

Amy was running her fingers round the edge of her folder, politely waiting for her turn to talk to Susanna, and hoping that she'd come in on the tail end of her conversation with Chris. In view of Susanna's upcoming trip back to the US, they needed to *firm up the plans so that she could book the flight* shortly, and *arrange the car service pick up time* accordingly. While waiting, Amy mentally reviewed all the *things that were running her late*, the *slew of e-mails* she was left with; Susanna's appointment with Sam to reschedule; David's hiring *contract to track down*; Dawn's request for a Blackberry. She was becoming mildly impatient. A shaft of sunlight came in the window illuminating millions of specks of dust and providing a welcome break from the dull light of a wintry day. Chris pulled out a chair for Amy, thus signalling that his conversation with Susanna was over and made his way out, calling "*I'll put my mind to it,* Susanna". Amy had been tempted to sidle out, but unless she dealt with Susanna's journey today, *it would hang over her* until it was done. They *wrapped up the details* of the trip in five minutes flat, and Amy left, satisfied that *everything checked out* and there were *no loose ends*.

The morning went by, as busy as ever. On the only rare occasions when Amy got out of her seat, she stole a look out of the window. With her thumb and forefinger, she inched apart the pale grey slats of the ropey Venetian blind. *Going outside chilled you to the bone*, as she'd realised coming in to work that morning, and now, it was almost as if snow was on its way. Something had been niggling her since mid-morning, and unconsciously caused her to prick up her ears once in a while: it wasn't as if her colleagues ever had any shortage of things to do, so why did the place feel so unusually quiet? She'd heard of no major event that would keep them away from their offices that particular day. Across the partition, she could hear Susanna complimenting her interlocutor: "*This is an excellent rundown, as I normally expect from you*, could you forward it to Chris as well?"

And then, it all came back to her; the first snowflakes she caught sight of triggered it. Already there was a light dusting of snow on the ground and memories of last year's gridlock came rushing back to her. Within hardly an hour, *traffic had been at a standstill* and *the transport system had collapsed*. Of course, living and working in Massachusetts, Susanna was unlikely to be fazed by a few snowflakes. Amy picked up the phone and called reception. Romain's familiar voice came: "Sorry, Ms Bird, there's no way I can reserve a taxi for you. *Due to the high volume of calls*, taxi companies are overwhelmed and aren't taking any more customers". Amy's hunch was confirmed. The sooner she got Susanna back and safe to her hotel in Paris, the better. She looked up the Mappy driving directions map on the internet. The whole Paris area was a tangle of red lines: *motorists were getting nowhere fast* obviously, and Susanna's 30 minute drive back might well turn out to be twice or three times as long. A firm believer in the notion that *one well-placed call can save a lot of hassle*, Amy decided that her next move was to turn to Mr Oliveira, her own trusted taxi driver. No luck there either. She was running short of options, and now not only *was the snow lying*, but it was snowing heavily. The kind of landscape that would have had the company Artists Club's budding painters reaching out for their paintbrushes, but which was sure to make life very difficult for workers who were *having an early finish*.

Amy even thought of calling Daserole drivers across the Atlantic, hoping against hope that because of their extensive network, they might oblige. As a matter of fact she did – to no avail. Time had passed, it was already past 4 pm; the few remaining colleagues had left in dribs and drabs. Amy pictured herself walking Susanna back to the station, up the steep, slippery slope and then on the crammed Paris RER and metro because she couldn't possibly leave her to brave them with so little practice of both the underground and the language!

But then, Kim showed up and Thomas, and Vinona, and Jonathan. They were coming out of a meeting and about to *look in on* Susanna. "*It's high time we pushed off*", one of them said, "they'll have to helicopter us out of here if we aren't careful". Amy sneaked looks at Susanna's low heel court shoes, unsure that they were well suited for cutting through new snow. But she was breathing a little more easily now. As the party were trudging their way up the slope to the RER station, a happy bunch of revellers who threatened to slip at every step and whose slightly excited voices echoed in the stilled, silent street, she couldn't help thinking that some people would pay good money to see this. **Strength in numbers** indeed!

GENTLENESS IS NOT WEAKNESS BUT RESTRAINED STRENGTH

His "Good morning" was a mere whisper. As he walked past Abigail's office, Remy was lost in thought; and by the look of him, sleep hadn't visited him the night before. Just now he was quietly cursing that he'd let himself *be roped into* this personnel representative job. He felt it fell to him to inform his colleagues of the impending closure of their Paris site. Much as he would have liked to *frame it all with more positive news*, the prospects were pretty grim. For many, it was going to be *a real kick in the teeth*. "Fancy a cup of coffee?" inquired Abigail, motioning him to the coffee machine. Remy forced a smile and introduced a positive tone into his voice. "*I certainly need a caffeine boost* this morning. Can't say no to a cup of coffee!" How could the management be so dismissive of the people at the receiving end of this major restructuring plan? How could they so blatantly tread on people's sensibilities like they did? It was bound to be *an emotive issue* and his would be an uphill task. First breaking the news – as long as nothing transpired before, and then negotiating with the trade-unions over the coming redundancy payments. That *was going to be a high wire act*. Not to mention the evening out with the top management scheduled for the following week. Remy had two crucial messages to pass on to them, which they might not be prepared to hear. And of course, it would be in nobody's interest if he *got on the wrong side* of them. "I was thinking, Remy, about our next company trip: how about we made some inquiries about Borneo as our next destination?" Abigail was asking as he fell into step beside her. "What about it indeed?" Remy thought glumly. "We've had two cancellations for our coming week-end in Prague, haven't we?" Remy was pleased he'd *dodged the question*, and, changing the subject, steamed right on with the conversation.

In the face of an industrial dispute this big, Remy's resources were finite. But he knew his contribution in the transition process could be significant. The restructuring wasn't about figures or about *cutting losses* while *reinforcing the company's claim on the future*: it was about men and women whose livelihood was taken away from them and who were now vulnerable to the uncertainties of a ruthless job market. They would need both time and paycheques that would free them from financial worries for a while. Those were the two messages he would relay to the *Head Honcho* when he'd be visiting next week. His twenty-five years in the company had made him *the living embodiment of its history*. He'd *had a ringside seat throughout its development* and now he was lead actor in its final act.

That Tuesday afternoon, Remy did face up to his new responsibilities. His stomach in knots and mindful that he had to tread carefully, he imparted the news that closure was imminent and that those who wouldn't be able to move to the new site in Strasburg were out of a job. Thankfully *he'd caught the mood of the assembly*; he could feel he had *defused a potentially severe crisis*. Emotions shouldn't cloud their judgement, including his, and they shouldn't *be led away from their goal,* which was that each single employee should get the best deal.

Responses to the news were bound to vary. With the size of his severance package and so close to retirement, Dominique would soon think all his Christmases had come home at once. Laura on the other hand, with her husband on the dole and her three children, would be among *the hardest hit*. There'd be the token moaners and their *constant carping*; those who'd *be fighting their own corner* indifferent to the interests of their colleagues; those who would be only too pleased to *fan the flames of* discontent. Now he *was in for the long haul* and in the months ahead he'd have to *chart a steady course through* troubled times indeed. He had embraced his mission with a not inconsiderable display of brainpower, but also with great empathy and tact. **Gentleness**, he knew, **is not weakness but restrained strength.**

LIFE IS EITHER DARING ADVENTURE OR NOTHING

A Land rover pulled out of a space, opening up a choice parking spot for Greg. He swerved into it, cranked up the handbrake and killed the engine. He was well ahead of himself, he knew, and had *arrived a full hour before Megumi and Hoshi were due*. At least, arriving *well in advance would allow for* whatever time was needed to get to the arrival hall, and negotiate the labyrinthine Terminal II multi-storey underground car park. "Hi, Charlotte! *It's all going to time*", he shouted into his mobile phone as he picked his way through the milling crowd. "I was expecting to *sit in traffic on the périphérique* to Charles de Gaulle, but it was free-flowing all the way". "You know what Neil McElroy said about airports?" Charlotte replied in her not unusual playful tone, "In the space age, man will be able to go around the world in two hours – one hour for flying and one hour to get to the airport. It seems you've beaten the record! Call me as soon as you've picked them up, we may have a few loose ends to tie up". Greg was used to gadding about airports, but *meeting and greeting* foreign guests, and holding *a sign with his name on it for easy identification* was a first! He was now absently watching the passengers drifting out of the arrival area, mentally rehearsing his schedule for the next two days and a half. Once he'd collected the two Japanese delegates, they'd be driving off directly to the company's headquarters, south of the capital, hoping to catch Olivier's opening speech in time.

The seminar *had gone ahead in spite of the short notice*. They'd had to *push key items off the agenda* due to the extremely tight timetable, and would have to *wrap up at 4 o'clock sharp* on the Friday, in time for the participants to taxi back to the airport – well, for those who had to fly back home, that is. The comforting thought was that he wouldn't be roped in to do the driving! Greg's phone trilled at the bottom of his inside jacket pocket. He rummaged for it and took Charlotte's call. As he did so, his parking ticket fell out. He picked it up and mechanically ran his eyes over the small print before putting it back in his pocket: Roissy, 30/03/11 A 11:45:53. "Greg", Charlotte was saying, *I'm going out of the door as we speak* and locking my office. Olivier says I'm needed at the HQ. I did tell him I was on a sun lounger, sipping Martinis and he'd have to wait, but he just pretended not to take the hint. Honestly, Greg, *what did his last servant die of*?! How about we beam him up and run the seminar without him? "Oh, come on Charlotte, *you're a gem*, you know that. You've done a great job organising the seminar. If it weren't for this irrepressible sense of humour of yours, *there wouldn't be enough gold stars in the world*! Greg's two guests were duly collected. No battles with parking meters to be fought, no traffic hold-ups. They were at the location on time, *signed in on arrival* and were immediately caught in the whirlwind of activities, plenary meetings, workshops, discussion groups. The fine balance between work and recreation was achieved, the food was excellent, the hotel arrangements perfect.

On the Friday morning just after breakfast, the fifty delegates trickled back into the main room and resumed their seats. They were still busy chatting, rebooting their computers, or already poring over graphics and data bases when a message *was called up* on the central screen for everyone to read. One by one, they looked up at it. The gentle hum of conversation soon broke into a buzz of excitement as the full meaning of the notice sank in. All heads were angled up now, transfixed by the message. The news was just plain bad. Frédérique was cursing under her breath that this would only enhance France's poor image as a strike-prone country, Tjhin was worried that *his visa would run out* and started fretting about his return to Indonesia. As for poor Greg, he couldn't believe he was in for a two-hour drive back to the airport yet again!

This is how it read:

WARNING NOTICE

The union of taxi drivers has called a strike and is taking industrial action over poor working conditions.

Transportation to both airports and train stations will therefore be severely disrupted today.

A. Members of the team will offer car sharing services to Paris Charles de Gaulle. See list.

B. For other destinations, local shopkeepers have come forward and offered to put their vans and pickups at our disposal. Those of you who need transportation are requested to contact the baker's, the grocer's and fishmonger's (today of all days). we are doing our utmost to make this alternative solution foolproof.

A smile flickered across Olivier's set expression; he had obviously worked out the clues and immediately seen through the hoax. Unperturbed he went on tapping away at his laptop. Meanwhile there was great commotion. Charlotte sidled out of the building, a little dazed at the impact of her April Fool day's prank and slightly overwhelmed by how well it had caught on.

When she came back in, and resumed her seat next to Tjhin, he leant forward and, as if letting her in on a little secret he said: "It's a joke, it's a joke. There isn't a strike!!"

Upholding tradition was commendable, but maybe not *Charlotte's best bet*! On the other hand, "**Life is either daring adventure or nothing**", she felt sure. She'd obviously chosen the former.

WHEN SOMETHING IS WORTH DOING, IT'S WORTH DOING WELL

Hillary's head lifted slowly into view from behind her desk, as she heard a booming voice cut through the hushed silence of the corridor. She'd been squatting there, out of sight for the past half hour methodically sorting the content of her drawers into piles and trying to *achieve some measure of order* in her new office. "*I've had it with printers jamming*! How long has this one been *on the blink*, Hilla... Blimey, Hillary! Is this some kind of war zone?" Matthew froze as he was about to come in the door. Boxes were stacked in piles on top of the desk, loose files were strewn over the window ledge waiting to be sorted, *the cupboards had been turned out* and *there wasn't a spare surface anywhere*! As a temping assistant, she'd been the interim owner of quite a few offices, but none had ever required such drastic action as Claudia's. "*If there are specific areas that you wish to be involved in, please let me know*" was one comment she could remember from her interview with the company's Human Resources director. Spring cleaning on that scale was certainly not the kind of 'area' that would immediately come to mind. "Mr McGuire", she said pleasantly, "it all comes down to the theory of maximum usage of available space". Hillary had only known her colleague sales manager a couple of days, so she played it safe and called him by his surname. "Well, you'll be lucky if you're done before the end of the week, Hillary, but this is sure to *win you a few Brownie points*! Good move!" Six weeks after Claudia had left *on sick leave*, her office had very conveniently become multipurpose: a depot for office supplies, a General delivery address holding unsorted mail for almost the entire floor, a storeroom for contracts awaiting signature or pending archiving, a haven for lost keys, and much more. Hillary could have sworn all important knowledge on tourism, travel operators and Company Package holidays was in there too! The sheer size of travel-related literature accumulated over the company's lifetime was mind-boggling: backup issues of travel catalogues; quotes from travel agencies; correspondence with group travel organisers; postcards. Hillary obviously *had her work cut out*. Wasn't her only option to *get out there and do what had to be done*? Now that she'd got *her mental to-do list into shape*, she could *start ticking tasks off* and *make headway.* Besides, no one on the team seemed to have planned on making time to introduce her to the job – a common enough pattern. The "lull before the storm" syndrome, as she knew all too well.

Hillary disappeared behind the desk again. The phone went off; she jumped to her feet, half expecting the call to be yet another query about a forthcoming trip to some faraway place or about season tickets for the Paris Opera House. Claudia was, by the look of it, the company's de facto travel agent. *Her time commitment to the works council must have been considerable*! Hillary picked up. "Hillary Jones, Tazina & Co, can I help?" She gave a quick sideways look at her notes on how to operate her VoIP phone, in case she'd have to *redirect the request to another number*. "Hi, Nathaly! Glad you're calling. Yes! The contracts *have come in from your site via the internal post*. I have followed your instructions to the letter. Isabelle still has to *fill me in on* what to do next, but everything is under control. Actually, there's been improvement since we last spoke: the technician's called in, he's configured my computer, *which is a step up from when I arrived*; it's now connected to the printer –not that it does much good since it seems to have a mind of its own. Nope! ERP Software not accessible, *I'm not yet signed in on all the systems*. It will come in good time, I know! Ok, Nathaly, bye for now!"

Sitting crossed-legged on her swivel chair and staring out of the window into the middle distance, Hillary drummed her fingers on her chin. It would be some time before *she got her bearings in the maze of* complex contract procedures and regulations. But *she'd grow into the job* soon enough. Once the basics were in place, *she could puzzle out the details* as she went along. That's what temping was all about. She worked her shoulders around. "My back's killing me" she said aloud. As if on cue, Matthew knocked at her open door. "Tea, coffee?" he said Hillary turned round, a lock of hair spilling into her face. "A nice cup of tea *wouldn't come amiss*!" Michael and Gaetan joined them and they were soon deep in conversation in front of the coffee machine on the ground floor. They were on first-name terms by now too. The event in Brussels which all the team attended – and the reason behind the deserted offices and hushed atmosphere on floor 1 – was a must.

The company was *in the driving seat on the market* worldwide, but in an age of social media, events like this one remained *an important plank in the company's networking strategy*. "Anyway, Hillary, when they're back they won't believe their eyes. You seem to be doing a great job of tidying up Claudia's office! "Hillary felt the corners of her mouth turning up in a pleased smile. She liked it when people heaped the extra praise on her.

By the end of the week, all the team members were hovering by her office door, peeking a look inside now that it was in apple pie order and fit for purpose. **When something is worth doing, it's worth doing well.**

EVEN THE BEST LAID PLANS CAN GO AWRY

Sarah stormed out of her office, and *made a beeline for* the front door. She ran down the two flights of stairs outside the building, taking the steps two at a time, sprinted along the flower beds in the courtyard, halted in her tracks to *scan her pass across the reader for the glass doors to slide open*, passed reception and arrived gasping for breath at the catering manager's office. "You don't mean that the whole thing is off?" she blurted trying to keep the quiver out of her voice as she enquired, and glad her breathlessness served to cover her confusion. "I can't think of any alternative, Mrs Dean", came the reply, "there is just no venue for the drinks party to be held, especially *at such short notice*". Mr Devere was obviously affecting a composure that he didn't feel: the amount of splendid food going to waste, the staff resources allocated to hosting the party and the refund that he was unlikely to obtain in full, were no exciting prospect. "*Profuse apologies*, Mr Devere, I do appreciate this is a major inconvenience. There's got to be a way, surely." This wasn't Sarah's finest hour, she should have known better than to *double book a room*. Mr Devere's phone call, five minutes earlier, hadn't half brought her up with a jolt! "Where did you say we were to lay out the food and drink, Mrs Dean?" he'd asked, "the place is taken up with a meeting all day." Despite her protestations about having done things by the rule book and to the place being booked in her name, Sarah was in for more disappointment and embarrassment. "Your reservation's been approved by R-Scheduler all right, but apparently it is made out for October next year, Mrs Dean, not October of this year!"

Sarah remembered how unusually and inexplicably easy it had been to *set up a date* for today's lunchtime party. The site was due to close before end of year and as building after building was emptied out, space was at a premium: even weeks ahead of the event all the available rooms *would be solidly booked* and *flexibility in choosing a date was bound to be very limited*. Well, it all made sense now. It said something for her scrupulous nature that Sarah had spent the hours leading up to the event checking on responses to the invitation, contacting the catering team to make sure everything would be delivered in quantity and on time, and generally *tying up loose ends*. Never in a month of Sundays would she have anticipated such an oversight!

Now, *time was romping away*, and there wasn't the slightest shadow of a solution in sight. "How about using the cafeteria?" Sarah offered. But this was immediately ruled out as the only available space was already spoken for. Both could see *this wasn't going to be an easy switch to make*. Mr Devere's level tone belied his anxiety. "I'll make a phone call", he said decisively, "see if I can get the keys to building K. It's completely unfurnished, but I could get the maintenance team to bring in a few tables. That might do the trick. We'd have to *allow sufficient time for the catering team to get from one end of the site to the other*, of course, and several trips, but at least it's worth a try. *I'll give you a shout* as soon as I know more." Sarah bared her teeth in as broad a smile as she could possibly muster, and thanked him abundantly.

As soon as she got confirmation that Mr Devere's idea was going ahead, she typed up a short text. It read "*Please note that the drinks party will now be held in room K 006*"and was sent as an update to all participants. She printed out two paper versions of the same, to be *posted on the meeting room doors* so that straying partiers would be redirected to the right location. The time was now approaching 12.30 and movement in the courtyard signalled that preparations for the cocktail were under way. *It was all systems go*. Sarah sat back in her swivel chair, lacing her fingers behind her head and breathing a sigh of relief at how things *were back on track* now that the crisis was over. *She had fallen behind with her work* somewhat, having had to leave aside matters related to the department's impending move. *People were counting on her to pass on vital and timely information*: the selective sorting of office documents, and the practical guidelines to *ensure the smooth running of* the transition. How to tag items of office equipment was equally important. In order for them to be safely routed to the new offices they must be reliably identified and properly labelled. She still had the afternoon ahead of her to follow up on the headphones. Now that most team members were going to work in open plan work spaces, they would be vital. Sarah was *glad they had everything squared away*. She could go back to *ticking tasks off* and *make headway with* her list of to-do things as long as your arm *in preparation for a busy next few days*. But just now, she was setting finger to keyboard again, typing a huge 'Thank You' in brightly coloured Word Art letters. They would be accompanying the box of chocolates she was determined to buy Mr Devere and his team as a token of *how indebted to them she was for* making the drinks party happen *against all odds*. **Even the best laid plans can go awry.** Forming a real partnership can go a long way towards making them work, though, and as a matter of fact, had saved the day.

AN IDEA IS WORTHLESS UNLESS YOU USE IT

Delegates from three continents had converged on that tiny little village, a mere dot on the map of the Greater Paris region. The "Domaine de Besalbel", was in the middle of nowhere, but offered its hosts remarkable surroundings, which, it was hoped, would make for a successful two days of both team building and high powered working sessions. After almost a year *of hard slog and dedication* to the new project, the teams badly *needed a shot in the arm* and this seminar aimed to *boost the energy levels* of all those so deeply involved in the project. Phone conversations, Web meetings and video-conferencing, were put on hold for a while, and virtual collaboration *kicked into the long grass* – for the duration, that is. Group dynamics, building trust and defining roles and goals were the order of the day. At this late point in the afternoon of 30 January Kirsty was running through her colour-coded to-do list. She was making sure *there were no loose ends*, aware that *she'd done twice her usual stint* lately but satisfied that everything *was taking shape nicely*, and refusing to bow to pressure. One item highlighted in green read: list-for-lift-to-airport. This could *be put on hold* until Friday morning, ahead of the mid afternoon finish, she thought. "Ms Ferguson, glad you made it early! I take it the rest of the party will be here shortly? We still have concerns that we haven't received your payment yet: I'm afraid there's still no sign of a credit transfer on our account. We are way past the deadline'. Kirsty wrinkled her nose and let out a long-suffering sigh. Just when she thought she *could freewheel a little*, bang went her peaceful ten minutes alone! The subject had given rise to some prickly conversation between her and her company's accountant. *Given the short timeframe*, Kirsty had enquired about *speeding up the purchase request approval*, hoping to *get it past the financial controller* swiftly and duly settle the bill. Delays in payment reflected poorly on the company and compromised future bookings with the catering establishment. The owner was being diplomatic about it, but she could detect a trace of annoyance in his voice. Hardly a week before, his accountant had been far blunter and threatened to cancel the whole event, sending Kirsty into a spin of panic.

The two days were a success. The *catering team, which was more than professional*, clearly had a hand in it. More generally, *the meeting was kept moving on schedule*, and the balance between intensive work and recreation was satisfactory. Some of the group building exercises produced the most hilarious songs and provided joyful moments; the food was superb; two of the outbuildings were steeped in history and had attracted a keen interest, and the bedrooms were sumptuous. The seminar had *achieved its stated objectives and then some*. Kirsty *felt a little out of her depth*, of course, since they were all blinding her with science, but judging from the sessions *she had sat in on*, it had gone a long way towards relieving stress. Both the workshops and plenary meetings had helped clarifying roles, articulating longer-term goals and sharing observations and concerns. The furrowed eyebrows and worried expressions of some had now disappeared.

Apart from the trifling matter of Patricia Robinson's last minute request for an off-the-menu dish, everything *had gone without a hitch*. Sam Bunn and Jaclyn had followed suit and been equally fussy with their food but, the catering team had kindly obliged. Kirsty thought that a fitting medium of respect for the staff's work wouldn't have gone amiss. She had, however, done a very good job of biting back a pointed remark. The badges (featuring the company's logo and colours) made *for easy identification* especially as *there was no seating plan*. Sadly, one badge had remained undelivered. Kirtsy reflected that it might, in fact, have been called the 'Badge of Courage'. Its recipient had declined and stayed behind in Canada, *very medicated* and heroically struggling against her illness. "We all know how indebted we are to Pam and her role in our Project. How about sending her a little something saying how much she's being missed?" Michel had spoken into the mike; "I was thinking along the lines of a booklet with messages of good cheer and everybody's signature in it, together with a photograph? This means of course, that before Friday afternoon, we'll have to *round everybody up for a good photo shoot*". The idea had instantly won wholehearted approval. For two days, writing pens and markers, glue sticks, coloured paper and card, self-stick coloured labels, and scissors were at people's disposal in the glassed-in seating area, off the main hall. Whether the delegates would stop by and indulge in a bit of handicraft was anybody's guess. Michel's idea had been ambitious: getting each and all to pause for a while in the course of their busy two days would certainly *take some doing*. Pointing them in the direction of the improvised workshop would be very much like *herding cats*. And yet, in spite of the *back to back meetings* and the overstretched timetable, people had been seen milling around the place. They were good humouredly giving their best shot at conveying their heartfelt sympathy and expressing their very best wishes to a dear colleague and friend. **An idea is worthless unless you use it.** Michel had used his and had done so advisedly. A Director of Human Resources with initiative.

CONCLUSION

One can overstress biography, but my twenty-three years of teaching experience as well as my linguistic background prompted me to take the hill less climbed and make new forays into business English. The corporate world, its mores and manners, its diverse sets of codes and practices, has been an interesting vantage point from which to gather evidence about how the English language is really used in business situations and to chronicle its on-going evolution. As the sheer bulk of this compendium shows, the bilingual assistant's remit is wide. The demands of the job, multi-faceted as it is, are high; so are demands to meet the linguistic needs that it generates. This verbal landscape filled with speech patterns and words offers an accurate picture of the work-place and recreates life behind the scenes in boardrooms and offices. It is hoped that by discovering the possibilities of an increased scope to express their own thoughts in a variety of contexts, users will enjoy the process.

GLOSSARY – GLOSSAIRE

A

above and beyond (go)
 se démener, 197

amiss (wouldn't go)
 ne serait pas de trop, 197

amiss (wouldn't have gone)
 n'aurait pas été de trop, 264

annoyance
 agacement, 263

appraise (to)
 mesurer, 250

armoury (an)
 arsenal, 82

assignment (an)
 mission, 82

avail (to no)
 en vain, 253

available
 disponible, 261

awareness (enhance people's)
 donner au personnel une conscience accrue (de leur valeur au sein de la société), 82

B

balls in the air (keep a lot of)
 faire plein de choses à la fois, 4

banter
 badinage, plaisanterie, 249

bared her teeth
 grimaça un sourire, 261

beam somebody up (to)
 emmener quelqu'un loin, téléporter, 256

belie (to)
 démentir, 261

bid to (in a)
 pour tenter de (diminuer le temps d'attente), 5

bite somebody's head off (to)
 rembarrer quelqu'un brutalement, 198

blimey
 Mince, alors ! J'y crois pas, 258

blurt (to)
 s'exclamer d'un trait, dire tout de go, 260

boardroom (a)
 salle de conférence, 4

bound (were bound to)
 ne manqueraient pas de, allaient sûrement (varier), 254

bow to pressure (to)
 céder aux pressions, 263

bulk of my database
 l'essentiel, la majeure partie de ma base de données, 2

bunch of revellers (a)
 bande de fêtards, 253

C

catering team (a)
 équipe de restauration, 261

chin
 menton, 259

CLERICAL (FUNCTIONS)
 administratives (fonctions), 5

clue (a)
 indice, 257

commendable
 louable, 257

compendium (a)
 recueil, 265

complaint coming your way
 une plainte qui vous pend au nez, 198

congenial
agréable, 248

corporate landscape (the)
le paysage, le contexte de l'entreprise, 2

crammed
bondé, 253

crop up, crisp and to the point (idioms)
les expressions idiomatiques émaillent le discours, savoureuses et percutantes, 122

cue (as if on)
fort à propos, tombant à point nommé, 259

curse (to)
jurer, pester, 253

D

daintily
délicatement, 248

dance attendance on (to)
être aux petits soins pour, 197

daring
audacieux, 257

daunted by
découragé par, s'étant laissé démonté par, 81

dazed (be)
étourdi, stupéfait, 257

deadlines
échéances, 121

deserve (to)
mériter, 197

diary constraints
contraintes de calendrier, 195

die in harness (to)
mourir à la tâche, 197

dignify with an answer
s'abaisser à répondre, 198

dismissive (of)
avoir (si) peu d'égard envers/pour, 253

dog's house (be in the)
ne pas être en odeur de sainteté, 198

doing my head in (he's)
il me prend la tête, 199

draw breath (to)
souffler, 251

drawer (a)
tiroir, 258

dribs and drabs (in)
par petits groupes, peu à peu, 253

drum one's fingers (to)
faire courir ses doigts, 259

E

eagerness
ardeur, empressement, 6

F

faffing around
brasser du vent/faire son cirque, 199

fair share to do (more than my)
plus que ma part de boulot, 198

fancy a cup of coffee?
ça te dit de prendre un café ?, 253

fazed (be)
se laisser décontenancer, 252

fiendishly
diaboliquement, 3

fired up (get people)
susciter l'enthousiasme des gens, 82

fitting medium of (a)
un minimum de (respect), 264

flat (in five minutes)
en cinq minutes pile, 251

folder (a)
chemise classeur, 251

follow suit (to)
faire de même, en faire autant, 264

forays (to make)
faire des incursions, 265

former (the)
la première option (l'aventure), 257

lull before the storm (the)
le calme avant la tempête, 259

M

merely walk-on role (a)
un simple rôle de figurant, 81

mike (a)
micro, 264

mill around (to)
s'activer, s'empresser, 264

milling
grouillante (foule), 255

mind-boggling
impressionnant, époustouflant, 258

minutes (to write)
écrire les minutes, 121

miraculous measure of order (achieve some)
arriver par miracle à un semblant d'ordre, 199

mistakenly
à tort, 81

moaners (the token)
les râleurs (de service), 255

muster
rassembler, 261

muster up the energy
trouver l'énergie, 198

N

niggle (to)
travailler, soucier, 252

no frills practical
sans fioriture et de base, 3

O

OD on (to)/Overdose on (to)
forcer sur, 249

one-liners
plaisanteries/bons mots, 248

open plan work spaces
'open space' (travailler en), 262

outbuildings (the)
dépendances (les), 263

overstress (to)
accorder trop d'importance à, 265

P

pattern (a common enough)
le scénario habituel, ce qui était assez caractéristique, 259

paycheque (a)
salaire, paie, 254

peek a look at (to)
jeter un coup d'oeil à, 260

pin number (conference)
code pour la conférence, 195

pore over (to)
étudier de près, être plongé dans, 257

prank (a)
farce, 257

premium (at a)
limité (espace), 260

prick up (to)
tendre, dresser (l'oreille), 252

prickly
épineux,délicat, 263

prowess
prouesse, 6

pull myself together (need to)
il faut que je me ressaisisse, 198

punishingly short timeframe
délais difficilement tenables, redoutablement difficiles à respecter, 5

Q

quiver (a)
tremblement, 260

R

redundancy payments
indemnités de licenciement, 254

S

storm out of (to)
sortir précipitamment de, 260

strewn (be)
joncher, être éparpillé sur (l'appui de la fenêtre), 258

strike-prone (be)
toujours disposé à faire grève, 256

strings of messages
un cortège de mails, 5

sun lounger (a)
chaise longue, 256

sweat blood (to)
suer sang et eau, 196

swerve into (to)
donner un tour de volant (pour s'insérer dans la place de parking), 255

swiftly
vite, promptement, 3

swivel chair (a)
fauteuil pivotant, 259, 262

T

take one step at a time (let's)
procédons par ordre, 197

take the hill less climbed (has prompted me to)
m'ont conduite à sortir des chemins battus, 265

take whatever's bugging him out on me (I'm not going to)
je ne vais pas le laisser passer sa mauvaise humeur sur moi, 198

ticking clock (the ominously)
le tic tac menaçant de l'horloge, l'inquiétant tic tac de l'horloge, 195

tidy up (to)
ranger, 260

tightly-knit programme (a)
programme serré, 195

tip-toe from one minefield to another
avançant prudemment d'un terrain miné à l' autre, 82

token of (as a)
en gage de (sa gratitude pour), 262

tongue stud
piercing sur la langue, 248

transfixed (be)
être cloué sur place, 256

tread on eggshells (to)
marcher sur des oeufs, 82

trick (might do the)
pourrait faire l'affaire, 261

trickle back (to)
revenir petit à petit, par petits groupes, 256

trier (a)
celui qui ne se décourage pas, qui est persévérant, 197

trifling
insignifiant, négligeable, 264

trigger something (to)
déclencher quelque chose, 252

trudge one's way up (to)
monter péniblement (la côte), 253

trying on the nerves (less)
moins éprouvant pour les nerfs, 196

U

unwieldy
peu maniable, pesant, 81

uphold (to)
maintenir, être fidèle à (la tradition), 257

V

valuable asset
précieux atout, 82

vantage point (a)
poste d'observation, 265

venue (no)
pas de salle disponible (pour le cocktail), 260

W

INDEX

A

B

C

D

I

J

K

L

Achevé d'imprimer en août 2013 par EMD S.A.S. – 53110 Lassay-les-Châteaux
N° d'impression : 28474 – Dépôt légal : août 2013

Imprimé en France